MOMBASA
AND THE KENYA COAST
A VISITOR'S GUIDE

First published by Evans Brothers (Kenya) Limited
PO Box 44536, 48 Shanzu Road
Nairobi

© Text John Jewell 1987
© Maps Evans Brothers Limited 1987
Maps devised and drawn by Jillian Luff.

All rights reserved. No part of this publication
may be reproduced, stored in a retrieval system
or transmitted, in any form or by any means,
electronic, mechanical, photocopying, recording
or otherwise, without the prior permission of
Evans Brothers Limited.

First published 1987
Reprinted 1988

US edition published 1988 by Hunter Publishing Inc
300 Raritan Center Parkway, CN94, Edison
N.J. 08818

Printed in Hong Kong by Dah Hua Printing Co Ltd

US ISBN 1-55650-069-6

MOMBASA
AND THE KENYA COAST
A VISITOR'S GUIDE

J.H.A.JEWELL

HUNTER PUBLISHING INC

Contents

Introduction vii

1. **Hints and Advice** 1
2. **History** 7
   Early history 8
   The Coastal civilization 8
   Afro-Asian culture and the growth of Coastal towns 9
   Vasco da Gama and the Portuguese conquest of the Coast 11
   The decline of Portuguese rule on the Coast 12
   Omani rule 13
   The slave trade and British and French interest in the East African Coast 14
   British rule 17
   Modern Mombasa 18
3. **People of the Coast** 19
   Africans 19
   Arabs 20
   Asians 21
   Europeans 22
4. **The Old Town** 23
5. **Fort Jesus and other places of interest** 29
   Fort Jesus 29
   Mbaraki Pillar 32
   The Mosque of Kilindini 32
   Fort St. Joseph (Sao José) 32
   Shehe Mvita's grave 33
   The Polytechnic 33
   The Tusks 34
6. **Mombasa Island and Town** 35
   Shopping 37
   The Town 37
   Exploring the Town 40
7. **Places of Worship** 45
   Christian churches 45
   Mosques 49
   Hindu temples 50
8. **Mainland North** 53
   Nyali Bridge 53
   Kisauni and Freretown 53
   The beaches 55
   Nyali Bridge to Mtwapa Bridge 57
   The Jumba Ruins and Takaungu 62
   Kilifi and Mnarani 63
9. **South Coast** 65
   The beaches and coral reefs 65
   Gazi village 70
   Msambweni and Ramisi 70
   Shimoni and Pemba Channel 72
   Wasini Island 73
   Kwale and the Shimba Hills 75
10. **Food: Be Adventurous!** 77

11. **Sports** 83

12. **Birds** 85
    Colourful birds 85
    Less colourful birds 89

13. **Trees and Flowering Shrubs** 93
    Trees 93
    Flowering Shrubs 100

14. **Suggested tours** 101
    Gedi 101
    Malindi 104
    Watamu 105
    Lamu 107
    Game park tours and lodges 108
    Voi Safari Lodge 109
    Taita Hills Lodge and Salt Lick 109
    Ngulia and Kilaguni Lodges 112

15. **A few Swahili words** 117

    Acknowledgements 120

Maps

Kenya vi
Migrations of peoples 7
The Portuguese occupation 11
Mombasa Old Town 23
Mombasa Island 35
Central Mombasa 38
The Coast north of Mombasa 54
The Coast south of Mombasa 66
Restaurants in Central Mombasa 78
Tours and game parks 102

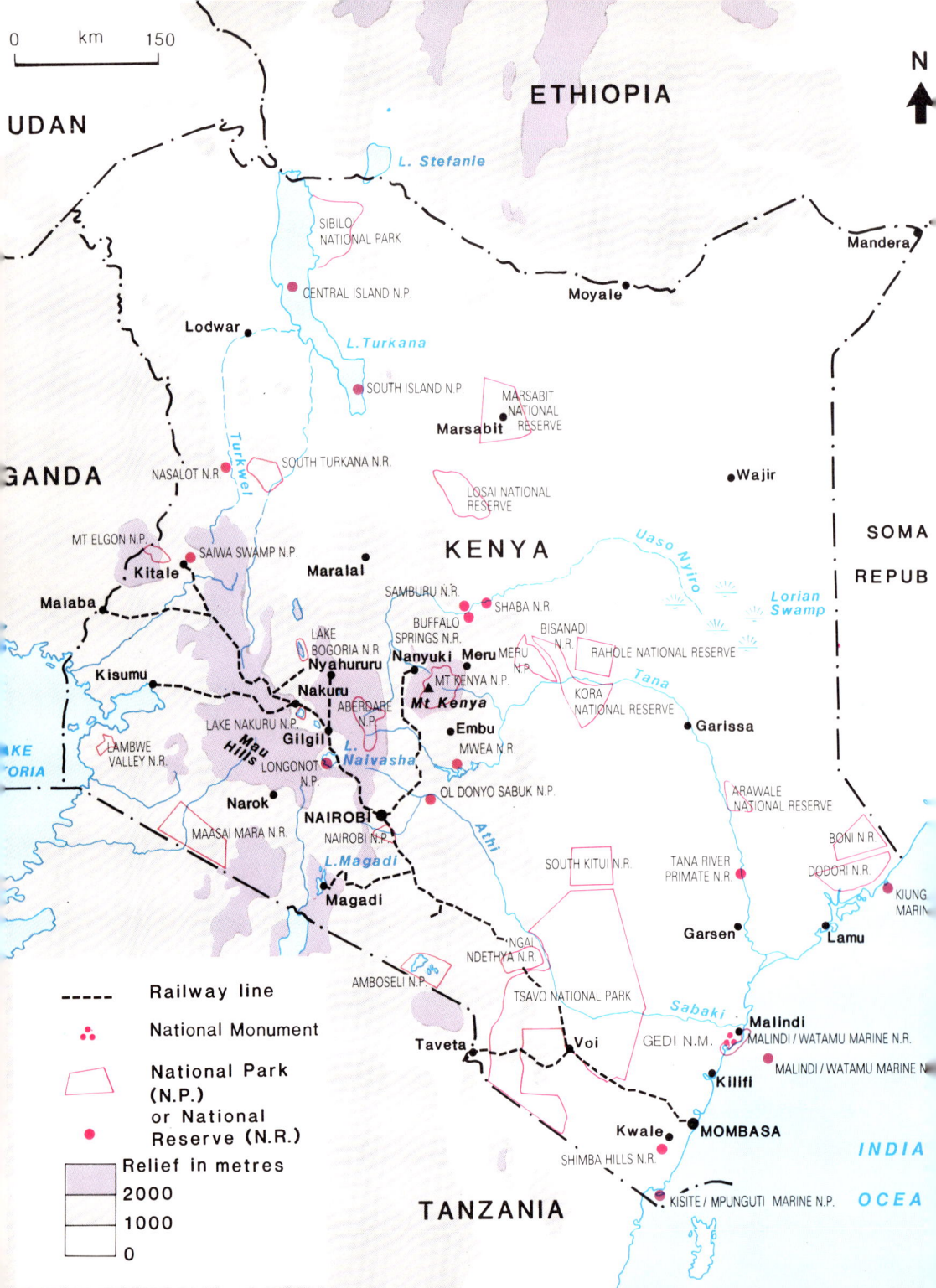

Introduction

KARIBUNI! Welcome to Kenya's magnificent Coast.

You are coming to, or perhaps have arrived at, one of the world's most colourful and spectacular resorts. The sea is azure blue; white rollers cream over the reef on to golden coral sand. Bougainvillea, flamboyants and hibiscus bring a riot of colour to your hotel garden. This is a veritable tropical paradise.

If you waken early you can watch the large, red globe of the sun coming up over the horizon, casting its roseate path over the sea straight towards you. Soon the sun is high, its colour changed to gold. Soaking up the sun and returning home with a glorious tan will make you the envy of your friends. But take time too to see something of Mombasa and its surroundings.

This book will help you to find your way about. It tells you where to go and what to see in Mombasa and the Old Town: how to shop, where to eat, where to go for sports and recreation. It suggests tours and day trips along the Coast and inland to watch birds and find African wildlife. And it tells you something of the peoples of the Coast: Africans, Arabs, Asians and Europeans live here; many of them have done so for centuries. Mombasa Old Town, with its narrow streets, exotic Arab architecture and bustling bazaars, and the ancient ruins along the Coast bear witness to a fascinating and turbulent past.

The deep water and safe harbours around Mombasa Island have attracted shipping for centuries and today Mombasa is Kenya's port and second only to Nairobi (a product of the twentieth century) in size and population. Recent years have seen a building boom along the Coast in both hotels and private houses. You would hardly believe that less than twenty years ago you could picnic on Mombasa beach and encounter just a few local fishermen coming at low tide to set their traps. There were no buildings between the beach and the Malindi road where there is now Mji Mpya, the 'new town', and the Mombasa Beach and Reef Hotels.

Today Mombasa offers you a large choice of hotels of international standard where you can hear a medley of languages. Most of the the hotel staff will understand English and you will quickly pick up the Swahili greetings: *Jambo, Jambo* ('How do you do?', 'I am quite well'); *Habari* ('What news?'), *Nzuri* ('Good news'). You will find a list of some of the most common Swahili words at the end of this book. Hints and advice for the visitor follow this introduction.

Enjoy your stay in Mombasa!

Central Mombasa showing area around the Sheikh Jundani Mosque

1. Hints and Advice

Arriving at the airport and departing at the end of your visit can bring some perplexing situations, hence the following observations.

You will be given a currency form on which you must declare the amount of foreign currency in your possession. Always change travellers' cheques at your hotel or a bureau de change where you will obtain an official stamp. This record will be examined on your departure. **Do not** engage in any currency deals, however favourable they may seem. If you are the victim of a double-dealer you will not find sympathy with the police. It is illegal to take Kenyan currency out of the country so make certain to exchange it before leaving. There is a bank at the airport for this purpose.

If on your arrival at the airport an official finds some article in your baggage 'dutiable', or some fictitious error in your documents about which you are unhappy, ask to see a senior official for clarification. Sometimes the problem will evaporate into thin air.

If you are not met by an hotel bus and need a taxi it is advisable to negotiate the fare before leaving. Many taxis have meters that do not work. Failing this ask at your hotel desk on arrival for the usual fare and bargain around it. Cars posing as taxis park along the busier streets so a kerbside pick-up is risky.

It is inadvisable to walk along deserted stretches of beach alone, especially at night, although this is a great temptation under a full moon. Unpleasant attacks have been known.

Should you need to contact the police, the Mombasa Police Headquarters are in Makadara Road near the Lotus Cinema. There are other stations in Jomo Kenyatta Road, Nyali, near the North Coast hotels and on the South coast at Diani. The telephone number of the Central Police and Provincial H.Q. is 311401 and the PO box number 90114. Do not expect an instant response if you are in trouble. Nyali Police Station telephone number is 471555 and the PO box number 90594. Diani Police Station telephone number is 01261 2121 and the PO box number is 40 Ukunda.

In the daytime carry just enough change to purchase a cool drink or buy some small article from one of the many beach

For a wide selection of cosmetics and perfumes

delial SUN PREPARATIONS
&
PRE-SUN PREPARATIONS
To Match Everyone's Sensitivity To The Sun

C. MEHTA & CO. LTD.
Dispensing Chemists

Established in 1933

Digo Road, P.O. Box 80314, Mombasa, Kenya
Telephone: 24706/21765
Opposite the General Post Office

vendors. Leave cheques and jewellery safely at your hotel. When in town for more serious shopping keep a purse or wallet in a safe place, not in a back pocket or a loosely-held handbag.

Most shops open at 8.00 a.m. and many remain open for business until 6.00 p.m. The lunch break is usually from 12.00 until 2.00 p.m. You will find a few smaller shops selling cold drinks and groceries which remain open even later.

There are usually few problems about photography and the shutter-bug has become an accepted hazard in the streets. However, many people, especially the Muslim community, are sensitive in this respect. It is as well to make your intentions known. In some cases a small tip is all that is needed, or, if you have a Polaroid camera, a present of the first picture will probably bring you willing models.

When in town try to dress in a modest fashion. Bikini tops and tiny shorts on ladies cause embarrassment in what is mainly a Muslim community. Because Mombasa is a holiday resort there is a lack of formality in dining rooms. Cotton material is the coolest wear, shorts (not too brief) and shirts being the most common gear. One sees many topless visitors on the beach but this is illegal and could carry a fine.

If you have any health problem it is as well to consult your own doctor before travelling. Bring with you any required medicines as some drugs in Kenya are sold under different proprietary names. It is advisable to take malaria prophylactics at least ten days before leaving your home and during your stay in Mombasa; continue ten days after departure to ensure against a delayed attack of fever. 'Paludrine' once daily or Lapudrine' once a week are satisfactory. They should be combined with one tablet of 'Fansidar' weekly. This regime is criticized by some doctors who feel it is safer to take no prophylactic. It is best to get the opinion of your own doctor.

Hotels usually have the telephone numbers of doctors willing to visit. There are three private hospitals in Mombasa with resident medical officers: the Mombasa Hospital, HH The Aga Khan Hospital and the Pandya Memorial Hospital, where you can receive medical attention at any time.

Should you have to enter hospital for treatment a problem may arise regarding payment, which will be requested before any patient leaves. Most visitors have a Health Insurance Policy but insufficient available cash, and this can cause embarrassment. It would be helpful if tour operators could have the authority to make the payments and reclaim later from the insurance company. There is a hospital tax in Kenya for residents but this does not help the tourist who will have to pay the full fees, and charges are high.

Some medical hints may be of value. At the Coast it is easy to forget how strong the sun can be; even swimming in dull weather can cause a sensitive skin to redden unless some care is taken. Use a sun-filter cream and stay in full sun for only short periods at first. Sunburn or heat exhaustion can ruin a holiday. 'UVstat' is a good ultraviolet ray filter; if you have a fair skin combine it with a tablet of 'Ro-A-Vit', a vitamin A preparation, for extra protection.

Stomach upsets can be very embarrassing, especially when on safari, and it is wise to have with you some 'Imodium' or 'Entrovioform' tablets. Drinking water is safe, but a strange diet and different kinds of fruit can affect the visitor in unexpected ways.

Allergies are fairly common in the tropics, so a tube of antihistamine cream to apply on rashes or insect bites is advisable. If you have the sort of skin that over-reacts to allergens a mild antihistamine tablet taken while symptons last will help.

Scratches and abrasions from coral are notoriously slow to heal. It is easy to strike your foot on a sharp coral outcrop while goggling so wear plastic shoes if you can. If you are scratched cleanse the affected area well and apply an antiseptic such as 'Mercurochrome'.

A century ago it would have been necessary to bring with you a large medicine chest on a visit to the tropics, but the items mentioned above will not take up much room in your baggage.

Trains leave Mombasa station at 5.00 p.m. and 7.00 p.m. for Nairobi arriving at 8.20 a.m. the following day.

Sleeping compartments are provided in first class coaches. There is a dining car and a well stocked bar, so dinner and breakfast are available. Bedding rolls are available and well worth while. They are arranged in position while you have dinner. The railway line runs close to the National Park as it nears Nairobi and you could be lucky enough to see some of the smaller game animals in the early morning.

The Kenya Bus Company runs, in conjuction with the Municipality, a regular service through the main areas of the island. In opposition to them are the minibuses or *matatus* which are privately operated and are usually overcrowded, the drivers take risks and the casualty rate is high.

Most hotels run their own service into town for the benefit of guests, and would be able to advise on reliable taxis. There are many car hire services and an international licence is all you require for self-drive.

A list of touring companies and car hire firms may also be useful. The following are members of the Mombasa and Coast Tourist Association. You can, of course, enquire at your hotel desk as to the most suitable for your purpose.

Across Africa Safaris, Moi Avenue. PO Box 82139.
    Tel. 315360/314394.
African Tours and Hotels, Moi Avenue. PO Box 90604.
    Tel. 23509/20627.
Airtour Suisse, Moi Avenue. PO Box 84198.
    Tel. 312565.
Archers Mombasa Ltd, Nkrumah Road. PO Box 84618.
    Tel. 25362/311884.
Avenue Motors, Moi Avenue. PO Box 83697.
    Tel. 25162/315111.
Avis Rent-a-Car, Moi Avenue. PO Box 84868.
    Tel. 23048/20465.
Big Five Tours and Safaris, Nkrumah Road. PO Box 86922.
    Tel. 311426/311524.
Coast Car Hire and Tours Ltd, Nkrumah Road. PO Box 99143.
    Tel. 311752/311225.
Diani Car Hire and Safaris, Ukunda, Diani Beach. PO Box 17, Ukunda, Diani.
    Tel. 2195.
Express Safaris Ltd, Moi Avenue. PO Box 86031.
    Tel. 25699.
Flamingo Tours (Coast) Ltd, Ambalal House, Nkrumah Road. PO Box 83321.
    Tel. 315635.
Globe Trotter Wales Cottages, Oleander Road. PO Box 81775, Diani.
    Tel. 2105.
Glory Car Hire Tours & Safaris, Moi Avenue. PO Box 85527.
    Tel. 313561.
Highways, PO Box 84787.
    Tel. 26886/20383.
Kuldips Touring Co., Moi Avenue. PO Box 82662.
    Tel. 25928/24067.
Leisure Car Hire and Tours and Safaris, Moi Avenue. PO Box 84902.
    Tel. 24704/314846.
Marajani Tours Ltd, Moi Avenue. PO Box 86103.
    Tel. 314935/315099.
Ocean Car Hire Ltd, Digo Road. PO Box 84798.
    Tel.313559/313083/23049.

HINTS AND ADVICE

Pollmans Tours & Safaris Ltd, Moi Avenue. PO Box 84198.
   Tel. 316732/3.
Private Safaris (E.A.) Ltd, Ambalal House, Nkrumah Road. PO Box 85722.
   Tel. 316684/5.
Rhino Safaris Ltd, Nkrumah Road. PO Box 83050.
   Tel. 311755/311141/311536.
Rusco Tours and Safaris Ltd, Maungano Road. PO Box 99162.
   Tel. 313664/21137.
Sawa Sawa Tours, Nkrumah Road. PO Box 80766.
   Tel. 313187/311479.
Southern Cross Safaris, Nkrumah Road. PO Box 90653.
   Tel. 311627/26765.
Sunny Safaris Ltd, Moi Avenue. PO Box 87049.
   Tel. 23578/20162
Thorn Trees Safaris Ltd, Nkrumah Road. PO Box 81953.
Transafrica Tours and Travel Services, Haile Selassie Road. PO Box 82929.
   Tel. 26928.
Turkana Safari (K), Moi Avenue. PO Box 99300.
   Tel. 21065.
United Touring Company, Moi Avenue. PO Box 84782.
   Tel. 316333/4.

Should you wish to contact your consul or high commission or their agents, your hotel desk will probably be able to supply you with the appropriate address or telephone number. The following are for quick reference:

Austrian Hon. Consul, PO Box 84045, Mombasa. Tel. 313386
Belgian Consul, PO Box 99697, Mombasa. Tel. 20231.
British Consular Representative, PO Box 90680, Mombasa. Tel. 25913.
Danish Consul, PO Box 95119, Mombasa. Tel. 316051.
Finnish Consul, PO Box 99543, Mombasa. Tel. 316051.
French Consul, PO Box 82804, Mombasa. Tel. 21008.
German Consul, PO Box 90171, Mombasa. Tel. 21273.
Greek Consul, PO Box 99211, Mombasa. Tel. 315478.
Indian Assistant Commissioner, PO Box 90614, Mombasa. Tel. 311051.
Italian Consul, PO Box 80033, Mombasa. Tel. 26948.
Netherlands Consul, PO Box 80301, Mombasa. Tel. 311043.
Norwegian Consul, PO Box 86954, Mombasa. Tel. 471771.
Rwanda Vice Consul, PO Box 87676, Mombasa. Tel. 20466.
Swedish Consul, PO Box 86408, Mombasa. Tel. 20501.
Swiss Consul, PO Box 84225, Mombasa. Tel. 316684.
USA Consul, PO Box 88079, Mombasa. Tel. 315101.

2. History

On 1 March 1498 three large ships appeared off the coast of Mozambique. They were Portuguese caravels which had sailed round the Cape of Good Hope under the command of the explorer-sailor Vasco da Gama in his search for the legendary kingdom of Prester John and lands across the Indian Ocean. These were the first Europeans to reach the Coast of East Africa and they found there a string of towns grown rich on the busy Indian Ocean trade in gold, ivory and slaves. The fourteenth and fifteenth centuries saw the flowering of the medieval Coastal culture and Mombasa was an important fortified town with many fine buildings.

But what of the early history of the Coast: who lived there and why was Mombasa important?

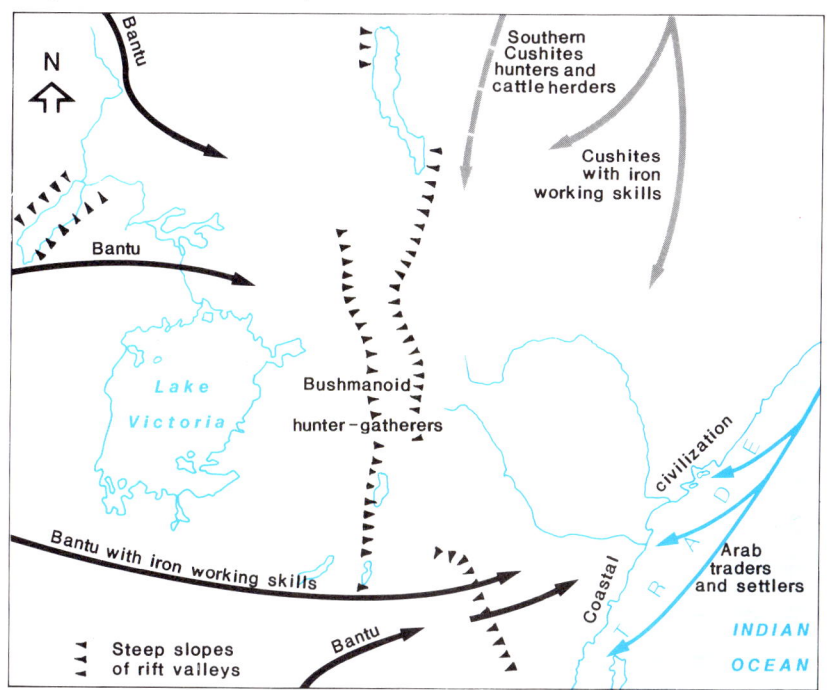

Migrations of peoples

7

Early history

The earliest inhabitants of East Africa, as far as is known, were Bushmanoid hunter-gatherers. Racially similar to the Bushmen of South Africa and Botswana they were Late Stone Age peoples who made and used tools of stone and bone. They lived by hunting and gathering wild plants, in the Kenyan and northern Tanzanian Highlands, the Rift Valley and on the shores of Lake Victoria. The next arrivals were also Stone Age men, probably Southern Cushites from what is now Ethiopia. They were hunters too, but they also kept cattle.

By about AD 400 the Iron Age was reaching East Africa. Other peoples arrived who could make iron implements which enabled them to cultivate the land and grow crops. This in turn allowed them to settle, and as they prospered and expanded so the hunter-gatherers and herders were forced out. The knowledge of iron-working had spread from Egypt to Meroe on the middle Nile by 500 BC, and to West Africa by 200 BC. The first iron-workers in East Africa may have been Cushites from the north or Bantu peoples from the west.

By AD 1000 large numbers of Bantu peoples were coming into East Africa. They apparently originated in central or western Africa and spread over the area in sporadic migrations over a period of hundreds of years. Some came into the north-west, intermingling with the Cushitic peoples; others came south of Lake Victoria and moved across the central Tanzanian plains to the coast. Here they spread northwards, driving out or absorbing the Bushmen and Cushites. A third wave of Bantu came into East Africa from the south-west, below Lake Tanganyika.

By the time the Bantu peoples reached the sea, however, a distinct Coastal civilization had emerged which was unlike anything existing in the rest of East Africa. It remained different and had little further contact with the interior for the next eight hundred years.

The Coastal civilization

Geography was responsible for the evolution of the Coastal civilization of East Africa. Cut off from the interior by mountain and highland regions and the steep escarpments of the eastern and western rift valleys, until the building of roads and railways people on the Coast looked not to the interior, but across the sea.

Early contacts with other civilizations were tremendously important to the history of the Coast and caused it to develop more rapidly than other regions.

The sand-fringed shore of the Coast between Mogadishu in Somalia and Sofala in Mozambique is broken by many inlets and harbours. Offshore are numerous islands, and some, like Lamu and Mombasa, are divided from the mainland only by narrow channels. It was around these harbours and islands that by AD 1000 the distinct Coastal civilization was growing up.

For hundreds of years the Coastal peoples had traded ivory, skins and slaves with Arabia and Persia. Merchants in their dhows visited the 'Land of Zanj' ('Land of the Black People'), as they called East Africa, between November and April, returning home from May to October, borne south-westwards towards Africa and then north-eastwards home by the prevailing monsoon winds. In due course some of these merchants settled along the African coast and on the islands.

Afro-Arab culture and the growth of Coastal towns

By AD 1000 many Arabs had settled on the East African coast. The merchants joined in the lively trade of the Indian Ocean, exchanging African ivory, gold and slaves for cloth and beads from Arabia and India; metal implements from Persia, Arabia, Syria and India; and silks and porcelain from the Chinese empire.

The Coastal town of Kilwa became important in the trade of gold (which came not from the Coast, but from about 400 kilometres – or 250 miles – inland, from modern Zimbabwe). Ivory reached the Coast at Kilwa and Mogadishu; and slaves were collected by Arab merchants at many points along the Coast, brought there by traders from the interior.

Over the years the merchants and rulers became rich and their wealth was reflected in their stone-built houses, palaces and mosques, which were mostly in Arabian and Persian styles. More and more settlers arrived and in the twelfth century most of the Coast settlements were founded. The next hundred years was a time of great Muslim expansion and many Africans were converted to the faith.

Gradually an Afro-Arab culture emerged. Racial mingling resulted in the Swahili people whose spoken language was basically Bantu, but with many Arabic words. The written

HISTORY

A 'Boom' at the Old Port with cement silos and Maritime Research Centre behind

language was Arabic for many years; Swahili was not an important written language until between the sixteenth and eighteenth centuries.

Kilwa maintained her position as the most important trading centre on the East Coast until about 1490 when Mombasa began to rival her. Having been a small settlement for the export of ivory and slaves for some 300 years, Mombasa now acquired sudden wealth and expanded. This may have been due to greatly increased trade with India. By the end of the fifteenth century Mombasa was transformed into a fortified town with many fine buildings. Its rulers were Swahili and it had a strong African element in its culture.

The fifteenth century was a time of great wealth and expansion; the more the towns prospered, the more settlers came from outside. The expansion might have gone on unchecked, but for the arrival of Vasco da Gama in 1498.

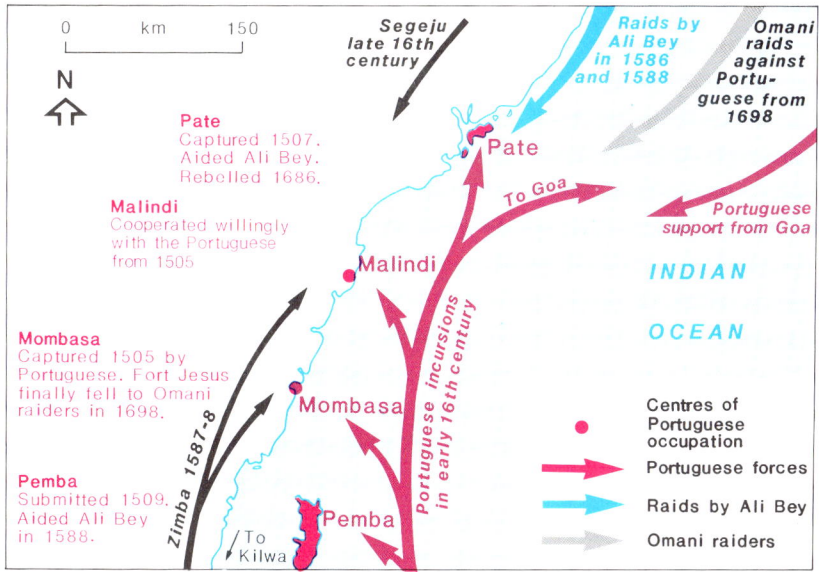

The Portuguese occupation

Vasco da Gama and the Portuguese conquest of the Coast

Vasco da Gama's journey round the Cape of Good Hope to lands so far not explored by Europeans was an historic one. As strangers they were not accorded the traditional hospitality, partly due to unfortunate incidents which raised insuperable religious barriers. Later the Portuguese, in their desire to enter the trade in luxuries from the East and to convert the Muslim lands to Christianity, needed a foothold on the East African coast. As Christians and rivals in trade they were not welcome, but they took advantage of the bitter rivalry existing between the Coastal rulers who were unable to unite to expel the enemy. By 1504 Portuguese attacks on harbours and shipping were seriously upsetting trade.

Kilwa and Mombasa were looted and laid waste and soon a large stretch of the Coast was under Portuguese rule. This state of affairs lasted for 200 years. The Portuguese were disliked and were unable to maintain control of the area. Trade declined and the period was one of decay. Mombasa, previously the wealthiest town on the Coast, resented occupation most, and in 1528 rebelled against the Portuguese. The rebellion was soon put down, however, and it was not until much later that the situation changed.

The decline of Portuguese rule on the Coast

In 1585 a Muslim Turk, Amir Ali Bey, promised the East African Coastal communities a *jihad* or holy war against the Christians. He succeeded in establishing his headquarters in Mombasa and prepared to destroy the only remaining Portuguese stronghold, Malindi. But reinforcements arrived to help the Portuguese, including a fierce, Bantu-speaking people from the south, the Zimba, who overran the island of Mombasa and might themselves have become a problem for the Portuguese had they not very soon been annihilated by the Segeju. (The Segeju and other Swahili peoples came to Mombasa from the north at about this time, because of Galla and Somali attacks on them.)

The Portuguese now took the defence of the Coast more seriously. The ruler of Malindi was made Sultan of Mombasa and in 1593 they built Fort Jesus and installed a permanent garrison of 100 soldiers. Their popularity did not increase, however. In 1631 the then Sultan led a bloody revolt against the garrison. He failed to oust the Portuguese, and for most of the remainder of the seventeenth century the towns of the East African coast were the battlegrounds of Portuguese and Omani soldiers and ships. The Imam of Oman lent his strength to the people of Mombasa.

The town of Mombasa was freed in 1660, but Fort Jesus was impregnable. In 1696 the ruler of Oman, Saif bin Sultan, brought over 3000 men to Mombasa and prepared for a long siege of Fort Jesus. It lasted thirty-three months before the Arabs finally broke in and captured the few remaining members of the garrison and the 2500 people who had taken refuge in the moat inland of the Fort.

The Portuguese managed to recapture Fort Jesus for eighteen months in 1728, but by then the Portuguese Empire had collapsed and they were finally expelled from the Coast of East Africa. Such was their subjects' dislike of them that they copied nothing from the Portuguese. Christianity made scarcely a mark on the Coastal civilization; there is no Portuguese influence in architecture, dress or customs. Perhaps the most positive result of Portuguese occupation was the introduction of new crops (mainly from the Americas) including maize, groundnuts, cassava, sweet potatoes, pineapples, paw-paw and guavas, some of which have since become staples for many Africans.

Omani rule

After the expulsion of the Portuguese the East Coast peoples doubtless hoped for a return to the peace and wealth of former days. But this was not to be. The Arabs no longer controlled the Indian Ocean and other Europeans, especially the French and British, were competing for its trade. The Omanis, having helped rid the Coastal towns of the Portuguese, took over as rulers of the East Coast. During the eighteenth and nineteenth centuries life in these towns was dominated by the struggles of the local people to free themselves from their Omani rulers and the struggles of the French and British in the Indian Ocean.

Once again rivalry between the Coastal towns prevented them from uniting against their enemies, and this time they turned to Britain and France for support. Oman was weak now and could make no more than the occasional effort to strengthen its hold on the East African Coast.

The last and most important attempt was the appointment in 1741 of a new governor to Mombasa which still led the struggle against the foreigners. The new man was chosen from one of Mombasa's oldest and most powerful Omani families, the Mazrui family, known as the Mazaria.

The Mazaria, however, soon established themselves as virtually independent rulers of Mombasa. Soon after the appointment of Muhammad bin Uthman al-Mazrui to the governorship, the Omani throne was seized by one Ahmad bin Said al-Busaidi. The governor refused allegiance to the new imam who therefore had him murdered and retook Fort Jesus. The next year the murdered governor's brother, Ali bin Uthman, recaptured the fortress and the town. Thus began a century of bitter feuding between the families of Busaidi and Mazrui.

The Mazaria extended their influence until by 1780 much of the Coast was in their hands. But only a few years later the governor was obliged to acknowledge the superiority of Oman. In the first decades of the nineteenth century they made two further attempts to challenge Oman, but in 1806 the most famous of the Busaidi Sultans, Seyyid Said, had seized power in Oman, and he soon expelled the Mazrui governor from Pate and supported the Governor of Zanzibar in successful attempts to liberate Pemba and Brava from Mazrui control. The final stages of the Busaidi-

Left: Stern view of a double-masted Boom. Small numbers of these dhows still visit Mombasa

Opposite: Mackinnon Market, off Digo Road, has many stalls selling fruit, vegetables and other commodities

Mazrui struggle were approaching and they were to involve the British and the French.

The slave trade and British and French interest in the East African Coast

During the eighteenth century slaves became the most important export from the Coast of East Africa. The Arab trade centred on Zanzibar and Kilwa was the main market place for the French. The Yao people kept the merchants supplied with slaves and further north the Nyika brought human merchandise to the Coast at Mombasa. By the end of the century there had begun a

process of internal slave raids which, within fifty years, emptied large areas of land between the Coast and Lake Malawi.

The French needed slaves for their possessions in India. They had many trading posts in India and by the mid-eighteenth century they seemed set to dominate the eastern trade routes. British expansion in India dashed their hopes and the French turned instead to East Africa and greatly increased their trade there. By the beginning of the nineteenth century the slave trade was expanding rapidly and was exceedingly profitable to everyone engaged in it.

The Omanis recognized the superior sea power of both Britain and France, and in 1799 had signed a treaty with Britain in which they agreed to keep the French away from their territories. In return they hoped for British assistance in defeating the Mazrui rulers of Mombasa.

Said bin Sultan, the new Imam of Muscat who came to be known as Seyyid Said, was unable to turn his attention to his African domains until 1822. Pate asked for his help to attack the Mazruis with the result that Pate and Pemba were occupied by Seyyid Said's forces, who then threatened Mombasa.

Two British naval vessels were occupied at this period with mapping the Coast. Sulaiman bin Ali, the Mazrui ruler, invited the British to assume control of his territory as a Protectorate. He must have considered this better than bearing the brunt of Seyyid Said's wrath. His invitation was unofficially accepted pending confirmation from London and so a short protectorate between 1824 and 1825 was established. The British flag was hoisted at the Fort. One of the ships involved was HMS Leven commanded by Captain Owen. A Lieut. Reitz was left ashore with a number of seamen, to administer the country. When Reitz died from malaria he was replaced by Midshipman Emery. Shortly afterwards the Protectorate was revoked by the British Government at Seyyid Said's request. Port Reitz and the Leven Steps in the Old Port remain to remind us of this period.

Seyyid Said was now determined to impose his rule on the Mazaria. He made two unsuccessful attempts and had to make terms with them. In 1837 he tried to persuade the governor to give up his post. This he would not do, but he did agree to an Omani garrison in Fort Jesus. Soon after, the Busaidi-Mazaria conflict came to an end, not by force, but by cunning. Some thirty members of the Mazaria were lured into the fortress, tied up and taken away by ship. They died in prison in the Persian Gulf.

Seyyid Said was now ruler of his East African dominions. To secure his position and to have closer control of an area that was growing richer all the time, he decided to move his capital from Mombasa to Zanzibar. This happened in 1840 and was the beginning of a new era in the history of the Coast.

It was not until 1873 that a treaty was signed which finally put an end to the slave trade on the East African Coast. And it was 1897 before slavery itself was abolished.

British rule

By this time Victorian explorers and missionaries had penetrated into East Africa beyond the Coast. The British government wanted to avoid colonial responsibility in East Africa while encouraging private traders. The race for the Upper Nile and German interests forced their hand, and in the late nineteenth century the scramble for Africa began.

In 1888 the British East Africa Association was reconstructed under royal charter and became the Imperial British East Africa Company. Two years later an Anglo-German agreement defined German and British spheres of influence and Germany accepted a British protectorate over Zanzibar and Pemba. In 1895 the Imperial British East Africa Company transferred its concession to the British Government, which established the British East Africa Protectorate to administer the ten-mile wide coastal strip rented from the Sultan of Zanzibar.

The Imperial British East Africa Company built stations along the Coast for administrative purposes and British political power and settlers soon extended inland. In 1896 work began on the Uganda Railway. The engineers overcame a variety of difficulties. Lions at Tsavo, the steep slopes of the Rift Valley and Nandi raiding parties were coped with and the railway reached Lake Victoria on December 26th 1901. The end of the line was known as Port Florence but this was later changed to Kisumu. Mombasa town gradually spread out of the harbour area, which came to be known as the Old Town, towards Kilindini, the new deep-water harbour, which could accommodate larger ships.

Increasing European settlement in up-country Kenya led to new businesses being established in Mombasa, and the ancient port became truly the 'Gateway to Kenya', as well as its capital. It was not until 1907 that Nairobi, which had grown from a collection of railway sheds and stores to a busy township, took over as capital of Kenya. By then roads and railways were being constructed to connect the Coast with centres inland and the Coast began to loose its distinct cultural identity.

Modern Mombasa

In 1928 Mombasa became a municipality. Its importance today is as the largest port in Kenya which was granted its independence from Britain in 1963. Mombasa boasts a large oil refinery and a cement works, and modern high-rise buildings have appeared on the skyline. The Old Town, however, remains much as it used to be: a symbol of the hardiness and resilience of its older communities.

Kilindini Harbour with ships alongside and Likoni ferry boats further away. Mombasa town is in the background

3. People of the Coast

Take a walk through the colourful, bustling streets of Mombasa and you will brush shoulders with Africans, Arabs, Asians and Europeans; they all bear witness to the long and fascinating history of the East African Coast.

Africans

Africans, of course, form by far the largest ethnic group: about three-quarters of the total population of present-day Mombasa. (At the time of writing, the total population within the municipal boundaries was about 600,000.) They are the oldest inhabitants of the Coast and something of the complicated story of early migrations of Bantu and Cushitic groups to the Coast is told in the previous chapter. There are so many different African peoples in and around Mombasa today that it is impossible to mention here more than a few.

Children in Old Kilindini Road

Of the non-Coastal peoples in Mombasa the largest group is the Akamba, followed by the Agikuyu, the Jaluo and the Taita. The Akamba come from an area midway between Mombasa and Nairobi and they make the wooden carvings of animals, birds and people which you will see on stalls along the streets.

The north-eastern Bantu live today in the Coast Province, and on the Coast itself are the Digo south of Mombasa and the Giriama who live between Mombasa and the Sabaki River. Much of the African dancing put on by the hotels in Mombasa is performed by Giriama girls in short skirts that swing out with the rapid movements of their hips. Akamba dancing is more acrobatic.

The Swahili, descendants of the early Afro-Arab traders, live today at the shipping and trading towns along the Coast: Kilifi, Malindi and Pate as well as Mombasa. They are made up of the 'Twelve Tribes', subdivided into the Miji Kenda or Tissa Taifa, and the Thelatha Taifa: the 'nine towns' and the 'three nations'. The Miji Kenda live mostly along the coast and the Thelatha Taifa are associated with the Island. They are proud of their individual status and each group still has its own *tamin*, or ruler, and elders. When the Coast was a part of the Sultanate of Zanzibar, the *Liwalis* (the Sultan's local governors) did not interfere with Swahili law and justice, which were highly respected.

Some of the beach hotels employ Maasai and Samburu warriors as guards. You may well see them, clad in a red cloth or *shuka* knotted over one shoulder, with plaited hair covered in a red ochre and coloured beads on their foreheads.

Arabs

Arabs were the first foreigners to visit the shores of East Africa. They came as traders and bearers of the Muslim religion and settled at places favourable for shipping which gradually grew up in sheikdoms. Mosques of different denominations are to be seen in Mombasa and all along the Coast, reflecting the variety of Arabs who settled here and their missionary fervour. They came originally from the Yemen and the Hadhramaut, in South Arabia, and later from Oman, Iran and the Gulf States. Today they form less than a tenth of the population of Mombasa.

Although many Arabs today wear European dress some still favour the *kanzu*, a full-length white garment (over which a short white or cream coat is frequently worn) and the Muslim *kofia* (cap).

Walking in the Old Town as sundown approaches you will see many Arabs gathering near the mosques, waiting for the call to prayer. The 'S' bend of Digo Road close to Biashara Street is a favourite meeting place at this time.

Asians

The Asians are the largest racial group after the Africans. Walk along any of the streets in town and look at the names over the shops... Gidoomal, Khandwalla, Sindh, Doshi etc. As in most of East Africa the Asians are traditionally traders. Many came in dhows on their seasonal visits starting in the mid-1800s, and some who had established themselves in Zanzibar during the Al Busaid period later moved to the mainland. Many came from the Punjab when the Uganda Railway project was started.

The majority come from the State of Gujerat and although several sects have their own language Gujerati is their lingua franca.

They fall into categories along religious lines, e.g. Muslim, Hindu, Parsi and Christians. Of the numerous Muslim sects, perhaps the Dawoodi Bohras form numerically the largest group, with Ismailis a close second. The Hindus have almost as many smaller sects. The Sikhs belong to a religious group on their own. Their Temple is on Mwembe Tayari Road with the popular Sikh Restaurant next door. The Parsis are also a small group and the sun plays an important part in their religion. In most of their temples elsewhere the sun is focused on the 'altar' at mid-day and fills the place with a bright light. The Goans are mostly Christian due mainly to the occupation of Goa by the Portuguese for some three hundred years. There is also a small group of Christians from Kerala in South India, one of the oldest groups of Christians in the world. You will probably visit the colourful Lord Shiva's Temple, the Jain Temple and the Swami Narayan Temple, and perhaps learn something of the intricacies of the Hindu religion. Lord Shiva's Temple is interdenominational under the Hindu Union.

Although the Asians came originally to trade, they are now in business of every kind, and in the professions. In sporting events Asians are often high on the list. Sikhs and Goans excel at hockey. Asian names appear amongst the top tennis and golf players.

H.H. The Aga Khan Hospital and the Pandya Memorial Clinic are the result of Asian enterprises, as are the Allidina Visram High

School (1918) and that of H.H. The Aga Khan.

Like the Arabs, many Asians have adopted European dress. But in Mombasa you will see Hindu women in saris, their menfolk in dhoti and Nehru cap. The Sikh turban is a common sight; Sikh and Punjabi women wear a loose blouse with baggy trousers gathered at the ankles. Bohra men dress in long coats with narrow white trousers; they are bearded and wear a Muslim cap. Their women wear the all-enveloping *rida* or *chador* in the streets. Muslims also wear a long, close-fitting blouse, a *kameez*, over *salvar*, (trousers), and a loose scarf around the neck.

Europeans

Walking along the streets of Mombasa today, especially during the high tourist season, you are likely to see many more visiting Europeans than locals.

Among the residents and citizens you will find many in the shipping companies, in businesses and in banking.

The British form the majority of the Europeans, and this stems from their original involvement in forming an administrative structure in the early days of the Protectorate and later Colony of Kenya. With this came a civil service and business people were quick to follow suit. Most up-country farmers have sold out and retired on the Coast. Some own cattle and fruit farms.

Shipping companies of many nations use the Port and have offices here, for example, Britain, France, the Netherlands, Germany, Italy and the Scandinavian countries. Airways of many nations also have representatives along the Coast.

You will find Italians running large engineering and construction companies. They are involved in the catering business and run many hotels; all the casinos are in their hands. Germans, too, run many coast hotels, the clientelle of which are largely German.

The Bamburi Cement Company has several Swiss and Germans who hold senior posts in the Company. The Dutch are involved in running the E.A. Oil Refinery. Banking is another of their interests. Most of the other European countries are represented in import/export businesses and small enterprises. There are Greeks in ships' chandling and the gem stone trade. Some senior posts in tourist offices are held by Europeans.

4. The Old Town

Mombasa Old Town is the cluster of houses and narrow streets around the Old Port. It extends from Fort Jesus to the promontory where the Allidina Visram High School stands and is bounded by the Abdel Nasser Road, Digo Road, Makadara Road and a short stretch of Nkrumah Road leading to the Fort. In aerial views of Mombasa the concentration of buildings of the Old Town stands out from the rest of the Island.

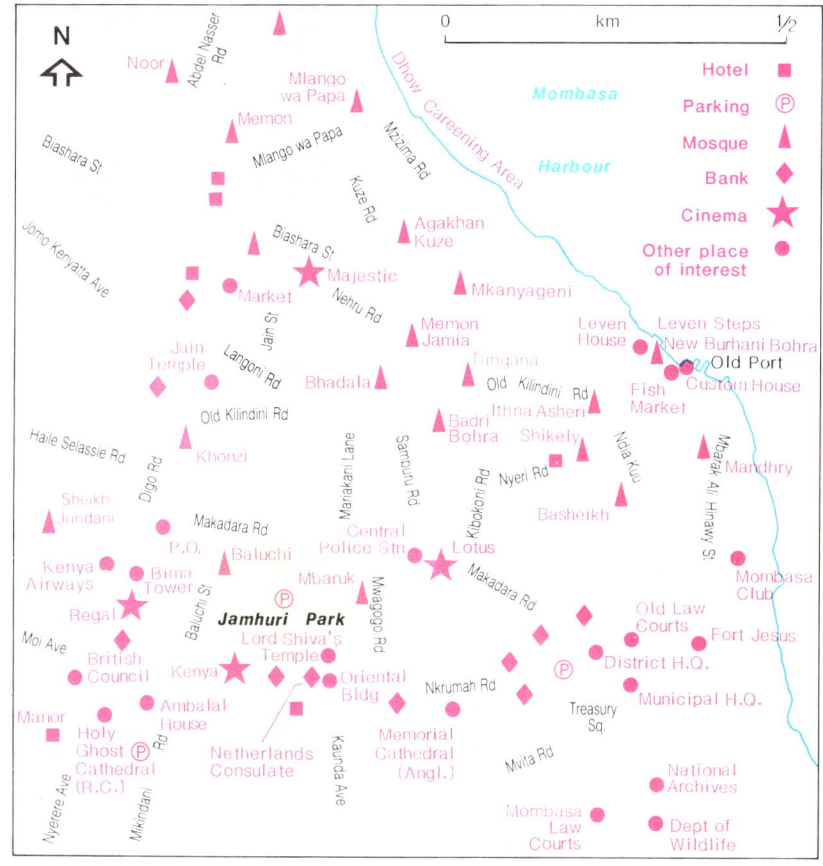

Mombasa Old Town

THE OLD TOWN

On an old map the Town of the Moors is separate from the Town of the Portuguese which is near the Fort. Between them is a sparsely populated area known as Kitovu, 'the navel'. The Moorish town was that of the Shirazi sultans, the last of whom was Shehe Mvita whose grave lies in the grounds of the Allidina Visram High School.

Historically one of the most important and busiest towns on the Coast, today Mombasa Old Town is disturbed only by the annual arrival of the dhows. It has its own quiet dignity. Yet down the narrow streets, behind the old facades, is a hive of activity. The Old Town is quite self-contained, with houses, markets, shops, business establishments, gold- and silversmiths, and nowadays small factories which make brass-studded and plated chests, deal with the attractive oyster shells imported from Oman and manufacture all sorts of brassware.

To walk down its streets is to enter another world. Going from the centre of the Island to the waterfront the streets become narrower: it is said they were made just wide enough for a loaded camel to pass. In some places you could reach from an upstairs balcony on one side of the road to the one opposite. The old woodwork is quite ornate and beautifully carved doves sit or hang from the supporting struts. During Portuguese attacks, the defenders apparently used to hurl down missiles from above. In less frequented parts of the Old Town there are still small houses of coral rag (large bricks cut out of soft coral and allowed to dry out to a hard consistency), looking much as they must have done in the time of the Mazaria and before.

Ndia Kuu, the main road, extends from the Fort to the dhow-careening area at Mlango wa Papa. Here people of all the nationalities of the Coast go about their business. The shops display a variety of Arab and Indian ornaments, carpets from Iran and Pakistan and carvings in local wood. Look carefully and you may find Arab silver anklets or a curved dagger in a highly decorated sheath. A visit to Ali's Curio Market is a must.

Mbarak Ali Hinawy Street joins the Fort with Government Square in the Old Port, a reminder that in the early days of colonial rule the British government offices were situated here. Sir Mbarak was the last but one Liwali of the Coast.

The **Mandhry Mosque,** near the bottom of the street, is probably the oldest of Mombasa's forty-nine mosques (*c.* 1570). Its distinctive white walls and minaret feature in many paintings and photographs. Its sect is strict Sunni.

On one side of the narrow street leading to **Government Square** is a refrigeration fish supply centre. There is a fish market beyond the square.

Near the top of the street on your left you will see a large garish painting on the outer wall of Anils Arcade, a large store selling dresses, material and other Africana. Almost opposite is Ebony, a store which sells carvings, copper and silver objets d'art and some valuable and interesting items. Next door is Sonals, with much the same to offer as Anils and further down the same street is another store, with a facade of Yemeni design.

At the junction of Ndia Kuu and Hinawy Street is a small, square shop (owned by the Timami family) which was once the Jubilee Hall, built to commemorate Queen Victoria's jubilee in 1895. *Barazas,* or official meetings, were held there.

At the bottom of the street **Government Square** opens out into the **Old Harbour.** Passing through the high gateway you enter the port, the **Custom House** to the left, storage sheds to the right. During the dhow season the Custom House used to be a fascinating place to visit: here you could see carpet upon carpet piled on the floor and beautiful brass-studded and plated chests. Nowadays very few carpets are brought in; chests are made locally and exported to the Gulf. You may see small coasters and Lamu *jahazis* (stoutly-built sailing boats) in the harbour. The numbers of large ocean-going dhows have fallen off considerably, although at the end of the northern monsoon in February and March several can be expected, trading with South Arabia and Somalia. Photography is forbidden in this area.

Beyond the Custom House where the street narrows is the **fish market** which functions each morning. Outside there is often an Arab coffee vendor with his conical brass coffee pot. From time to time he clinks together two empty cups in his hand to draw attention to his presence.

On from the fish market there is a good view of the harbour and the other side of the creek. The cement silos and, further up stream, the **Bahari Fishing Club** stand out, with the **Tamarind Restaurant** between them.

Continuing in the same direction you come to the new **Burhani Bohra Mosque** with its tall minaret. This is the third mosque to be built on the same site by the Bohra community, and is a landmark when looking towards the harbour from the other side of the creek.

Beyond this mosque is the site of **Leven House** where

Lieutenant Reitz lived during the short British Protectorate of Mazrui times. The location of Reitz's grave is not known. Nor indeed is the site of the Portuguese cathedral where he is thought to have been buried; but a family living in the Old Town, near where Old Kilindini Road joins Ndia Kuu, claims to see frequently an apparition of a young European man. Perhaps James Reitz walks again near his grave!

Below Leven House is the jetty, now so neglected that the corrugated roof has entirely rusted away. Immediately behind the jetty, within 15 metres of the sea, is a sweet water well which used to supply the dhows and is now a popular laundry site. **Leven Steps** connect the jetty with the area above and goods from the dhows used to be carried up them for customs inspection.

Going on up the harbour is the old fish market which used to flourish during the dhow seasons. Dried and salted fish were manhandled up from small boats at the foot of the steep cliff. There was a daily auction conducted mainly in Arabic. Sadly the area is slowly crumbling away and now it is difficult to recognize the building.

Further on is **Mlango wa Papa,** 'the sharks' gateway'. Here on the open beach, during the spring tides, the dhows would careen in preparation for their return journey to the Gulf. The large beach is known as **Pwaa Kuu.** Beyond this, and overlooking the beach, is the **Dhobi Ghatt,** a colourful sight on laundry days.

In the centre of the Old Town is a triangular area known as **Piggot Place,** at the junction of Nehru Road and Kibokoni Road. Here are many small shops and dwellings, and you may find a silver or goldsmith willing to make up jewellery to your own design.

There are several mosques in this area, including the Basheikh or **Tangana Mosque** on **Old Kilindini Road** which has a minaret similar to the Mandhry Mosque and some fine old wooden doors. The **Jamat-Khana** or Kuze Mosque of the Ismaili community at the Mlango wa Papa end of the road is one of the largest buildings in the Old Town and is prominent when viewing the Island from across the creek.

In Old Kilindini Road, between Samburu and Kibokoni Roads, is another Bohra mosque with a large, beautifully carved wooden door. Scattered about this area of the town are a number of more recent mosques. The **Bhadala Mosque** in Samburu Road is of more recent design. Close by is the **Memon Jamia Mosque,** with a colourful dome, which celebrated its centenary in 1980.

One of the most attractive Hindu temples is the **Jain Temple**

Left: Biashara Street, noted for its display of colourful kangas and kikois

Below: Making halwa, an Arab sweetmeat similar to Turkish Delight

ht: Fruit in plenty at one of the many s

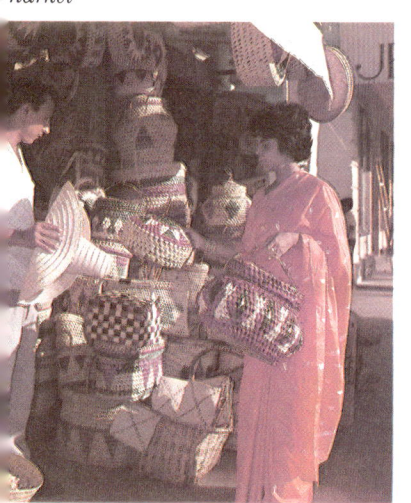

w: A Goan lady at a basket shop near market

27

which belongs to the Visa Oshwal community. A striking white building, approached by a short stairway guarded by two impressive black elephants with their *mahouts* (elephant keepers), it is situated off Langoni Road which enters the Old Town near Mackinnon Market.

Mackinnon Market is at the northern edge of the Old Town on **Abdel Nasser Road.** It sells fruit and vegetables and was named after Sir William Mackinnon, a founder of the British East Africa Association. Next to it is an open butchery and behind it are fascinating spice shops. Facing the main road are basketware shops which are well worth looking at.

Famous **Biashara Street** is mainly outside the Old Town, but starts in the region of the **Kuze Mosque** and crosses Abdel Nasser Road at the start of the 'S' bend. It is a must for every visitor, for here you capture the atmosphere of the Orient as you stroll down the narrow road, materials and dresses of all colours waving gently in the breeze.

If you have not tasted *halwa,* the 'Turkish Delight' of the Coast, get some now. You can buy it in a shop in Langoni Road, just beyond the Jain Temple. It is also sold in shops off the 'S' bend.

During the Muslim holy month of Ramadan, the pavements opposite the Mackinnon Market and extending round the 'S' bend are covered by small stalls selling vegetable and dates, *samosas* and kebabs. Buyers throng the stalls in the late afternoon to prepare for breaking the fast after sundown. Coconuts are piled high and you may slake your thirst with their milk.

5. Fort Jesus and other places of interest

Fort Jesus

Dominating Mombasa Harbour and commanding a view of ships entering and leaving the port is Fort Jesus, whose walls rise some fifty feet from a two-acre coral platform. Dedicated in 1593, and virtually completed three years later, it is today one of the best-preserved monuments on the East African Coast and one of the finest examples of a fort built in the sixteenth or seventeenth centuries. It was opened to the public as a museum in 1958 as part of the Kenya National Parks.

The walls of the Fort are up to almost 2.5 metres (8 feet) thick and there are four bastions, two on the seaward side, two facing inland. Their names commemorate famous men of the sixteenth century: Mateus for Mateus Mendes de Vasconcellos, the first governor of the Fort; Matias for Matias Albuquerque who was then Viceroy of India; Phelipe for the King of Spain and Portugal; and Albert for Albert the Pious, Archbishop of Toledo. Their coats of arms adorn the bastions. The seaward bastions of St Mateus and St Matias slope backwards from the central wall and would have been protected by enfilade from it. The landward bastions were so constructed that they provided cover for each other and the wall between them. They also protected the moat. For hundred of years Fort Jesus was impregnable.

On the seaward side of the Fort a large rectangular wall projects forwards from the bastions. At the foot of this wall is an old entrance which was used to bring in supplies and troops from ships anchored in the harbour. One of these ships, the *Santo Antonio de Tanna* which was sunk just off the Fort, has been investigated by archaeologists and many of its guns and the other contents have been brought to the surface and are preserved in the Fort's museum.

Visitors to the Fort climb the fairly steep approach, the elliptical bastion to their left, and enter through the heavy main gate. Over this gate is an inscription in Portuguese to Francisco de Seixas de Cabreira, the Commander in 1635, describing his

FORT JESUS AND OTHER PLACES OF INTEREST

deeds and the honours he received. There is an English translation on the left-hand wall, just inside the main gate. It makes rather grim reading.

Turning right you go through another gate to the flat rectangular area of the inside of the Fort. The ticket barrier and bookshop confront you. Across the open central area is the museum, where a barracks once stood. Another troops barracks stood along the wall to the right. On the left are the remains of the Captain's house; the church and cistern are to the right.

The museum is well worth a visit. On the covered patio are models of the *Mtepe* and *Dau la Mtepe,* ancient sailing craft, as well as some old doors. Inside are the finds from the wreck of the *Santo Antonio de Tanna* and a variety of pottery sherds and other archaeological finds.

A walk around the ramparts will help you relive the grim times of old and will reward you with fine views of the harbour entrance. A small enclosed look-out above the centre of the wall facing the Old Town was positioned so that a wary eye might be kept on the activities of the Mazrui governor.

An Arab house has been opened at the site of the cavalier bastion of St Antonio which is part of the bastion of St Phelipe. Here there are interesting exhibits from Oman.

Fort Jesus, guarding the entrance to Mombasa Old Port

Left: The leaning Pillar at Mbaraki

Below: Old door preserved at Fort Jesus

Above: The Water Gate, an old entrance to the Fort area. The white wall is part of the Mombasa Club swimming pool

Left: Visitors on the ramparts of Fort Jesus

Since its construction in the sixteenth century Fort Jesus has played a prominent role in the history of Mombasa. This is outlined in the first chapter of this book. Further information is given in the *Guide to Fort Jesus* and in the works of James Kirkman, the first curator of the museum.

Mbaraki Pillar

The leaning pillar of Mbaraki near Mbaraki Creek, where ship repair yards dominate the waterfront, is said to be the tomb of a Sheikh of the Changamwe, one of the original twelve tribes of Mombasa. It dates from about the late 1600s and there are mosque ruins nearby. A tall, conical structure of coral rag and limestone plaster, it rises from a square, hollow podium, its sides pierced with 'arrow slits'.

Its height has caused some speculation that it was used as a beacon for shipping entering the harbour, but this is unlikely since rising land and trees would obstruct such a light.

The pillar is phallic in shape and is said to be the scene of nocturnal rituals to aid infertile women and revenge acts of treachery. Lighted candles and gifts of fruit can often be found under the baobab tree nearby.

The Mosque of Kilindini

Built in the seventeenth century the Mosque of Kilindini, the so-called 'Wailing Mosque', was the main mosque of the 'Three Tribes' of Mombasa. It is on Liwatoni Road, off Tangana Road, near a branch line of the railway which crosses Moi Avenue and turns towards the Mbaraki Godown area. Some years ago there was not much left of the mosque: a large mango tree grew out of its centre and only parts of the wall remained. But in 1977 a new mosque, with brown walls, a low dome and crenelations along the top of the walls replaced the old ruins. The original high dome collapsed and was replaced by the present low one.

Fort St Joseph (Sao José)

Fort St Joseph (Sao José) was part of the Portuguese line of defence along the Kizingo sea front. Today it occupies a central position on the seaward edge of Mombasa Golf Course, but only a wall or two remain. The Fort was destroyed by shells from an Arab warship that ran aground on the reef opposite and stuck fast in such a position that the guns on the bow were accurately trained on the Fort. The defenders abandoned it as soon as the first cannon ball struck home.

There were other forts at Ras Serani near to what is now the end of the Golf Course, close to the sixth green.

Shehe Mvita's grave

Early Swahili settlement on the Island was mainly in the area between the old Nyali Pontoon Bridge and Mlango wa Papa, and on the land opposite Ras Kisauni further up the creek. The last Sheikh before the Portuguese occupied the area close to where the Fort was to be built was Shehe Mvita. His grave lies in front of the Allidina Visram High School. He is still revered and each year a special procession and dances take place near the grave. An old mosque ruin and graveyard lie close by between the road leading to the old Nyali Bridge and the creek.

An early dynasty, that of Mwana Mkisi, occupied the land where the Lady Grigg Hospital and the Coast Province General Hospital now stand and included land along Tom Mboya Avenue to the Hindu Crematorium. Tom Mboya Avenue was relaid when the new Nyali Bridge was completed, and a number of archaeological finds were made relating to Mwana Mkisi's era.

The Polytechnic

The change of name was inevitable. This attractive group of buildings of obvious Arabic or Moorish architecture started life as the Mombasa Institute of Muslim Education. It was opened in 1950, the cost of it borne by the British Government, by generous gifts from the majority of Muslim communities on the Island and from certain important personalities. The green-doomed Yusufi Mosque was named after its main contributor.

Originally the Institute provided a technical education in a variety of skills and trades for children of the Muslim communities. Nowadays there is no bar to entry apart from the attainment of a set standard of education.

During term-time it would be wise to make enquiries whether permission to see around has been granted.

The Tusks

On Moi Avenue, half-way along one side of Uhuru Gardens, four giant tusks arch over the road. These are now Mombasa's hallmark.

The Tusks were erected for the visit to Mombasa of Princess Margaret in 1956, in addition to the triumphal arch elsewhere where the Royal and the Mombasa coats of arms hung. The Municipal Council felt that a second arch would befit the occasion, and the Town Treasurer's suggestion that the two pairs of tusks on the obverse side of a 10-cent piece would make a topical archway was taken up by the Council.

Two large pairs of tusks were made up out of canvas on wooden frames by the municipal Engineers Department and erected on Kilindini Road, now Moi Avenue, at its junction with White Fathers Road. Such was the impression they made that the Council decided they should become a permanent feature of the town. They were reconstructed in aluminium and put in their present position a short while later.

The famous Tusks on Moi Avenue, Mombasa, next to Uhuru Gardens

6. Mombasa Island and Town

The Island of Mombasa is roughly oval in shape, nearly 5 kilometres (about 3½ miles) long and over 3 kilometres (about 2½ miles) wide. It is a kaleidoscope of colours and never fails to impress the visitor, whatever his or her interests may be.

Some will be intrigued by the architecture of the Muslim mosques and the colourful Hindu temples, others by the vibrant street life. No one could fail to be delighted by the beauty of the trees and shrubs along the mains roads: bougainvillea of many colours; the rich orange of the Nandi flame tree – especially on Nyerere Avenue; the flamboyants outside the Holy Ghost Cathedral and the large, shady banyan trees. The shops and bazaars will arouse your curiosity; their owners will lure you in with sweet words.

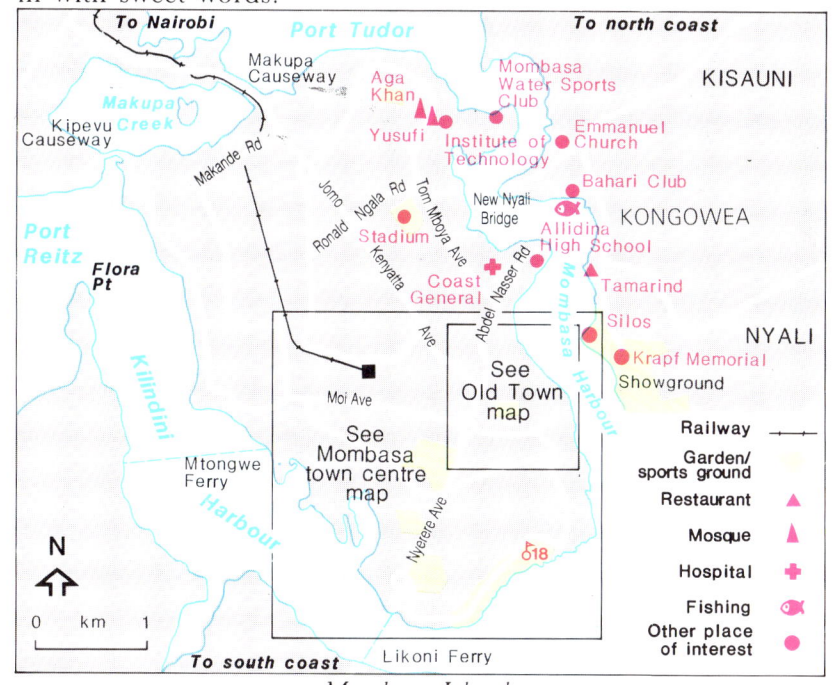

Mombasa Island

THE CITY BOOKSHOP LTD.

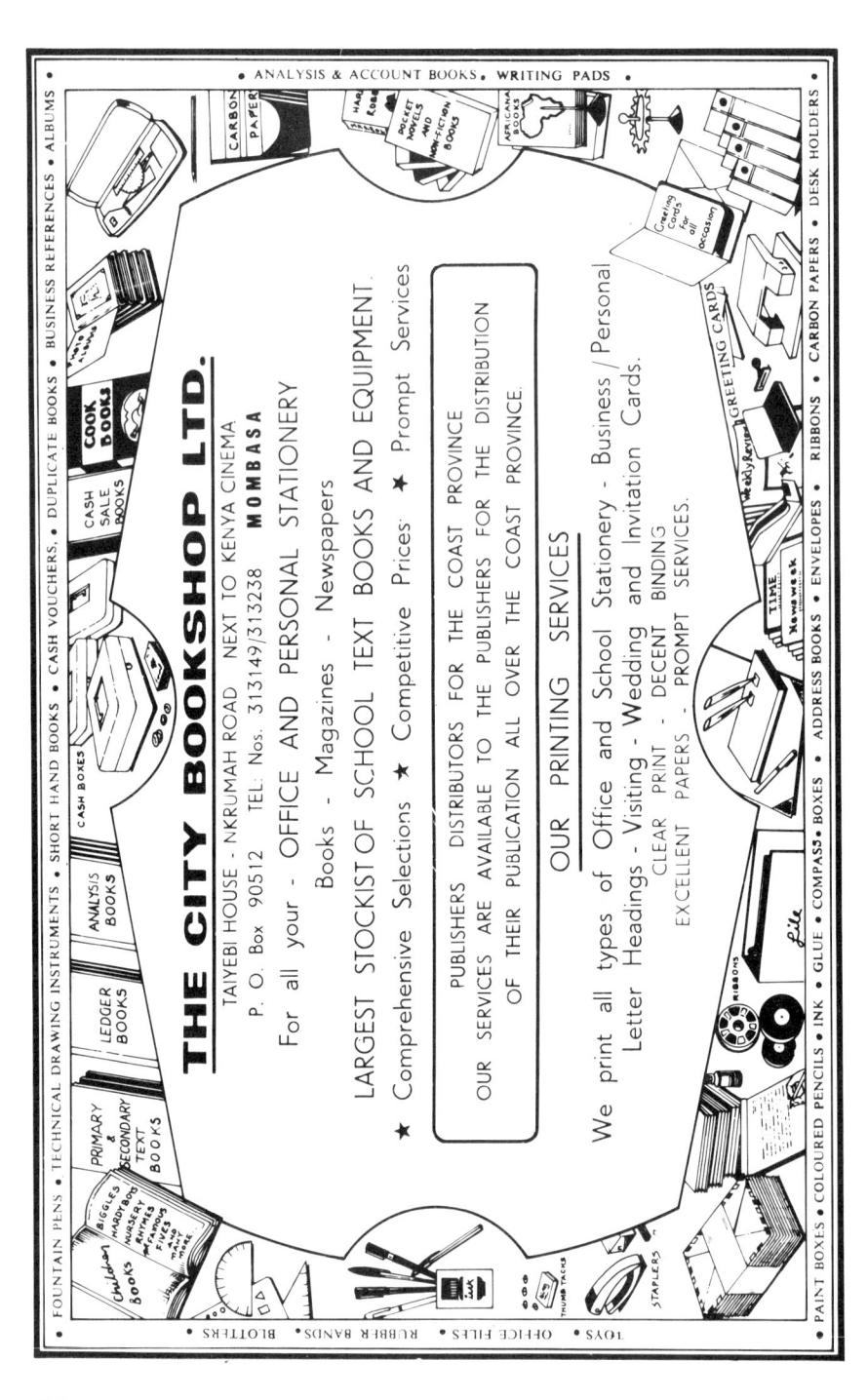

TAIYEBI HOUSE - NKRUMAH ROAD NEXT TO KENYA CINEMA
P. O. Box 90512   TEL: Nos. 313149/313238   **MOMBASA**

For all your - OFFICE AND PERSONAL STATIONERY
Books - Magazines - Newspapers

LARGEST STOCKIST OF SCHOOL TEXT BOOKS AND EQUIPMENT.

★ Comprehensive Selections ★ Competitive Prices ★ Prompt Services

PUBLISHERS DISTRIBUTORS FOR THE COAST PROVINCE
OUR SERVICES ARE AVAILABLE TO THE PUBLISHERS FOR THE DISTRIBUTION
OF THEIR PUBLICATION ALL OVER THE COAST PROVINCE.

OUR PRINTING SERVICES

We print all types of Office and School Stationery - Business / Personal
Letter Headings - Visiting - Wedding and Invitation Cards.
CLEAR PRINT - DECENT BINDING
EXCELLENT PAPERS - PROMPT SERVICES.

Shopping

The centre of the town is at the junction of **Digo Road** leading into Nyerere Avenue and Moi Avenue leading to Nkrumah Road. The best shops are here and visitors staying at the beach hotel are often brought to the Castle and Manor Hotels to do their shopping.

Some shops specialize in exotic local and Indian goods; others in the more fashionable local materials and dresses. Should you wish to purchase gemstones, several shops deal exclusively in this trade. Beth International can be relied upon to give you a fair deal. The pavements along most of the main streets are lined with small African stalls selling a great variety of goods, from soapstone chess sets to the popular sisal shopping bag, or *kiondo*.

There are so many shops offering such a wealth of merchandise that it is impossible to recommend where to go for particular things. It is best to 'shop around' and compare quality and prices before you make up your mind. This is the Eastern way of making an important purchase, and the shopkeepers will not be offended by your discrimination.

The Town

A glance at the map will show how the major roads fan out from this central point to divide the town into 'quarters'. We must go back a century to appreciate how the new town developed from the Old Town.

A writer in 1890 recorded that outside the town (the Old Town) there were only footpaths leading through the forest which was infested by puff adders. The widest path, just over 1 metre (about 4 feet) across, led to Kilindini, the 'place of deep water' in Kiswahili.

When the British took over the administration and ships carrying heavy cargoes arrived, the old dhow port and its narrow streets were unable to cope. A new harbour was essential and Kilindini was the natural choice. It was already used by dhows unloading goods for the villages on that side of the Island, and when construction of the Uganda Railway was about to begin, rolling stock and heavy stores were landed on the beach at Kilindini.

So began the building of this main road, Kilindini Road, followed by others around the seaboard of the Island as houses for administrative officials, and later the European Hospital, were

MOMBASA ISLAND AND TOWN

built. The first railway station was sited on flat ground behind the Fort and trolley lines were laid from the Old Town along the new roads. Uniformed trolley boys used to push the trolleys up and down these lines.

An open square near the station, now a pleasant garden, has a white, domed building in one corner which covers an ancient well. In another corner of the square the Treasury was constructed and today the area is known as Treasury Square Gardens. On one side of the square, in Mvita Road is the Ivory Room where elephant tusks were once stored for auction; several 'godowns' or storage sheds were built to be near the station. This area also contained the municipal headquarters, the town hall and various banks. The colonial architecture of the early

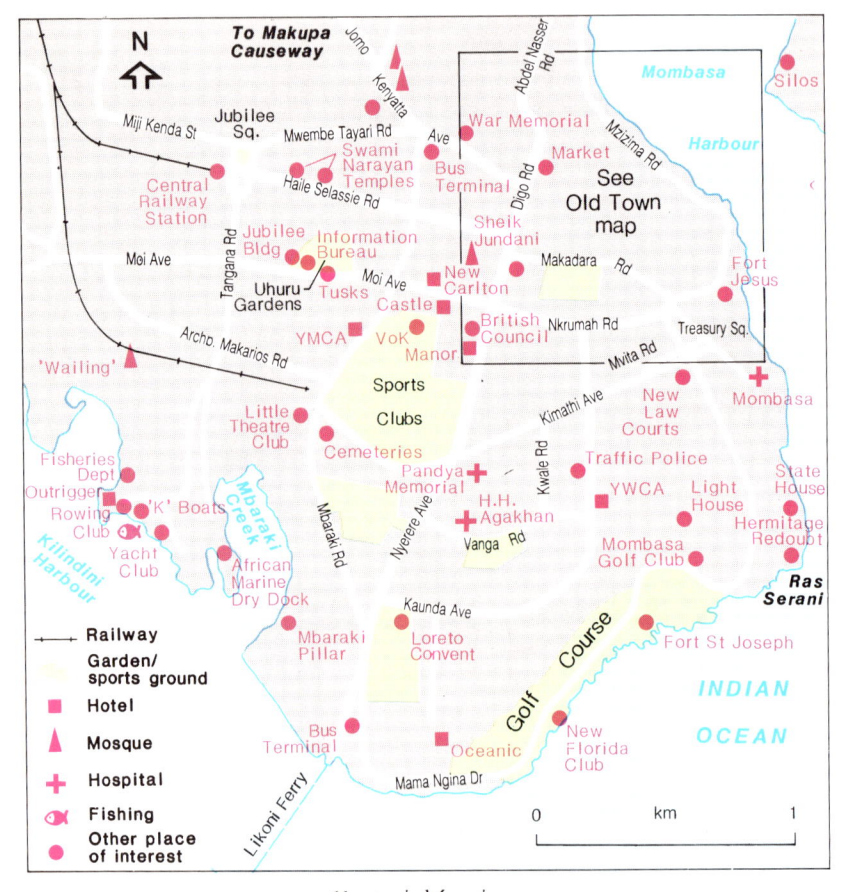

Central Mombasa

Opposite: The Likoni ferry crossing at sundown

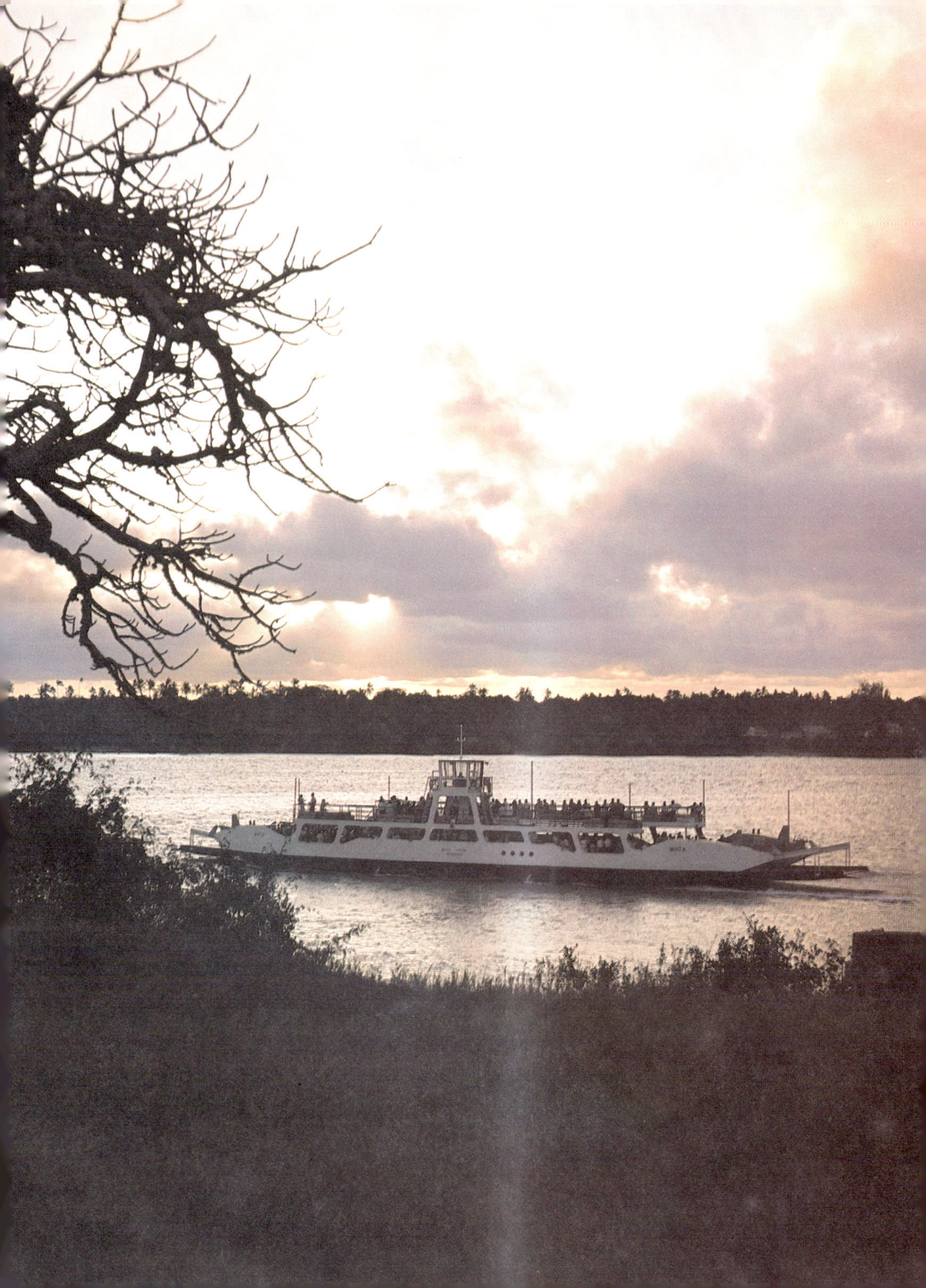

buildings contrasts sharply with the newly constructed Standard Bank and the prestigious Central Bank of Kenya.

As Kilindini developed many business houses moved closer to the new harbour. Shipping companies built offices near the docks, and in 1933 a new railway station was built, to be nearer the new Port. Then came a road from the Old Town to the station, originally Station Road, but since renamed Haile Selassie Road. Before long the Island was intersected by a network of connecting roads.

Exploring the Town

From the central roundabout let us start by exploring **Nkrumah Road.** The **Holy Ghost Cathedral** is on your right as you walk towards Treasury Square. The modern **Ambalal House** complex is beyond the Cathedral and dwarfs it. It houses a coffee shop, a restaurant and the **Cave Night Club,** besides travel agencies, boutiques, doctors' consulting rooms and offices. Further down the road, on the opposite side, is the **Kenya Cinema, Barclays Bank** and **Oriental Building**, where you will find the **Indian High Commission.** Then, on the right-hand side of the road, is the **Memorial Cathedral.** Passing Treasury Square and the banks, go on down the hill and you come to the **Old High Court** on your right and then to **Fort Jesus.** At the end of Nkrumah Road is the **Mombasa Club,** commonly called the Chini Club (*chini* is a Swahili word meaning 'below' or 'under'), which is the oldest club in Kenya. From here there are roads into the Old Town.

From Treasury Square, Mama Ngina Drive takes you to the seafront. The first large building on the left is the **Provincial Headquarters,** on the seaward side of which is the **Mombasa Hospital.** The new High Court buildings are on the right as you start to go down Mama Ngina Drive. **State House** comes next on your left. This used to be Government House, and in the days of the trolleys the Commissioner's House.

Continue along the sea front with its magnificent views of the Indian Ocean and you will pass the **Mombasa Golf Club.** Inland, to your right, is the lighthouse, an important landmark for ships entering Kilindini Harbour. Further on is the **New Florida Night Club** on the cliff edge and beyond that the **Oceanic Hotel** dominates the high ground on your right. Both the club and the hotel have casinos. The road continues through to a **Kenya Bus terminal** and the **Likoni Ferry** which will take you across to the south mainland. On Sunday evenings the Asian communities gather on the sea front beyond the Florida to enjoy the cool breezes and meet their friends. There are many stalls selling coconuts, samosa, roast corn and other delicacies.

A few baobab trees remain from what was once a forest. Legend has it that each Portuguese soldier was buried with a baobab seed in his grave. It is unlikely that the forest originated in this way, but the area was once the site of a very old village and there are many superstitions about the baobab tree. Without leaves it looks as if its roots are reaching for the sky. Herons nest in a sizeable heronry here.

Turn right at the end of the sea-front road and you will join **Nyerere Avenue** which takes you past the **Loreto Convent** and other schools, **Extelcoms House** and the old **Manor Hotel** back to your starting point. This hotel, one of the first in Mombasa, has a large terrace where cool drinks and snacks may be bought. Here too is **City House,** on the first floor of which is the **British Council** with its excellent library and reference room. As there is no longer a British High Commission in Mombasa, it is here that you may seek advice. (See list of Consuls etc. on page 6.)

Back at the junction in the town centre you can set off again down **Moi Avenue,** the old Kilindini Road, which goes to **Kilindini docks.** You pass the old-established **Zanzibar Curio Shop** before reaching the **Castle Hotel.** Here there is a covered patio which is a popular meeting place for tourists who come to sip cool drinks and watch the passers-by. At the hotel you will find tour agencies and a fine pizzaria. The taxi ranks are nearby. Moi Avenue is a dual carriageway and has a great number of boutiques on either side as well as shops selling gemstones and copperware. Opposite the Castle Hotel, street traders will offer you African paintings, soapstone carvings and colourful sisal bags. You can see the bags being made: African women often sit making them while they wait for customers.

Further down the road, beyond the **New Carlton Hotel** and the **Skyways Hotel** is the **Kenya Coffee House** where you can buy freshly-ground beans or simply drink the delicious coffee. Continue along the road and you will see the famous ornamental **Tusks,** two pairs arching across the carriageways. Behind the line of pavement stalls is Uhuru Gardens with its pleasant shade trees and a small pond, the centre of which is raised and shaped like a relief map of Africa. Next to the Gardens is the **Information Bureau,** whose staff are very helpful, and behind it are the Red

Cross headquarters and Koblenz Hall. Across the road behind the Bella Vista Restaurant is the new Reinsurance Plaza, with a busy supermarket on the ground floor.

Next comes the **Jubilee Building,** built to commemorate the golden jubilee of the last Aga Khan. It now accommodates several business premises, workshops and Government offices. The UTC building and other travel agencies are to be found on both sides of this road. Continue past the next roundabout and you pass the **Hong Kong Restaurant,** the first Chinese restaurant in town. This brings you to the mainly industrial area; here are the large motor companies and service stations. Dominating the area are two new high-rise buildings, Cotts House and Cannon Towers.

The road leads on under a railway bridge, the letters KUR (Kenya Uganda Railway), 1927, marked on its side. In early days it was nicknamed Putney Bridge. From here it is a short walk to the **Mission to Seamen** building with its facilities for visiting sailors; this overlooks the entrance to the harbour. The main industrial area is to the right, behind the harbour.

In the quarter between Moi Avenue and the entrance to Kilindini Harbour are the **Custom House** and the **Voice of Kenya**

Municipal Headquarters, Treasury Square Gardens

Above: A hockey match at Mombasa Sports Club
Above right: The Yacht Club

complex with its tall microwave tower. Here too are many sports grounds, including **Mombasa Sports Club** which caters for tennis, bowls, cricket, hockey, rugby and squash.

The road leading past the Mombasa Sports Club is **Mnazi Moja** (one coconut tree) and it becomes **Mbaraki Road** after a left turn separating the sports club from a cemetery. Opposite is the **Little Theatre Club** which puts on many excellent amateur performances. Turning right by an old baobab tree a small road leads you through a residential area to **Nyerere Avenue.** It is along here that you will see the leaning **Mbaraki Pillar.** Excavations have revealed the site of an old mosque, but little is known of it.

Close to the start of this road you can see the **African Marine Dry Docks** across **Mbaraki Creek.** Near the Likoni Ferry are large cement silos; berths for ships line the waterfront. Most of the ships come in for cement, but visiting naval vessels are often berthed here too. Looking up the harbour you can see the **Yacht Club,** one of the older clubs of Mombasa with a fine record of sailing, the **Rowing Club** and the **Outrigger Hotel** which caters for the deep-sea fisherman. Beyond is an area largely taken up by the Fishing Department. You then pass ten deep-water berths before reaching the oil jetty, and the large storage tanks of Shimanzi nearby. At Kipevu, on the mainland, there is another jetty for crude oil which is transported by pipeline to the oil refineries at Changamwe.

Kilindini Harbour is separated from **Port Reitz** by a narrow spit of land extending northwards from Mtongwe on the mainland, and the **Kenya Naval Headquarters,** to Flora Point.

To complete the town tour take **Digo Road** leading away from the central roundabout where we started. Bima Tower and the Post Office dominate the road on the right. Opposite Bima Tower is a bus stop with the Kenya Airways Office at the corner. If you go up Gusii Street, you will see the **Sheikh Jundani Mosque,** an attractive building set in an enclosure partly shaded by coconut palms. Around this area are hardware stores, restaurants and minimarkets.

The next turning left off Digo Road is **Haile Selassie Road** which leads to the **Railway Station.** Here are the Sikh Temple, the Sikh Restaurant and the two Swami Narayan temples, one of which is very colourful and has an entrance door made up of painted panels, each showing one of the reincarnations of the Lord Krishna. Opposite this temple is the Patel Samaj community centre, behind which, on Agakhan Road, is the main community centre of the Ismailis. An oval garden separates Haile Selassie Road from the railway station.

Turn left at the roundabout near the markets and you come into **Jomo Kenyatta Avenue** which extends as far as the Makupa Causeway. First you will pass through a market area. The headquarters of the **Kenya Bus Company** are on the left; the **Native War Memorial** and a Muslim burial ground are on the right. Further on the road is bordered by shops and filling stations.

The area of the Island to the north of Jomo Kenyatta Avenue is mainly residential. It also contains the **Municipal Stadium,** the **Polytechnic** and several schools. Tom Mboya Avenue curves around the waterfront on **Tudor Creek** and Ronald Ngala Road splits it in two between Jomo Kenyatta Avenue and the new **Nyali Bridge.** The Hindu crematorium with its interesting gate and the **Coast Province General Hospital** are in the area between the creek, Tom Mboya Avenue and Abdel Nasser Road. You will probably go along these roads if you are taken to see the new Nyali Bridge from the centre of the town.

7. Places of Worship

Most readers of this guidebook will be from Europe and the western world. But the visitor may be interested to look at the mosques and temples, as well as Christian places of worship. Being essentially a Muslim township with quite a sizeable Hindu population, Mombasa has many fine examples of these religious styles of architecture.

Christian churches

The Memorial Cathedral

This is the Anglican Cathedral of Mombasa and is one of the oldest Christian churches in East Africa. Approaching Treasury Square down Nkrumah Road it is on your right. Its large silver dome, cruciform shape and arched entrances give it a Middle Eastern appearance which is in keeping with the Old Town.

The Cathedral was built by the Church Missionary Society in memory of Bishop Hannington (who was murdered on the Uganda border after a long foot safari to meet the Kabaka of Buganda), Bishop Parker and the Reverend Henry Wright, the Society's secretary. It was consecrated in May 1905 by Bishop Peel, under whose direction it was built. Brass plaques at the side of the chancel tell something of the story of these four men, and in the nave more plaques commemorate early pioneers.

At the eastern end of the cathedral is a fine rose window. Opposite it, at the western end, a circular window depicts some of the visions of St John. High stone pillars and an impressive stone pulpit give an air of spaciousness. Hannington's own wooden chair of local make remains in the cathedral and has been used for the consecration of all the bishops of Mombasa. The organ, acquired at a cost of about £1700 in 1931, was for a long time the finest in the country.

Until 1884 the Church in East Africa was part of the diocese of Mauritius. When it was established, the Diocese of Mombasa covered not only present day Kenya and Uganda, but large parts of Tanzania as well. Services are held in both Swahili and English.

PLACES OF WORSHIP

Opposite, top right: Door at the Bohra Mosque, Old Kilindini Road

Right: Baluchi Mosque, on the side of Jamhuri Park

Below: The Holy Ghost Cathedral

Right: Jamhuri Park with Lord Shiva's Temple right centre and domed bandstand in centre

Opposite right: The sacred bull gazing at the sanctuary in Lord Shiva's Temple

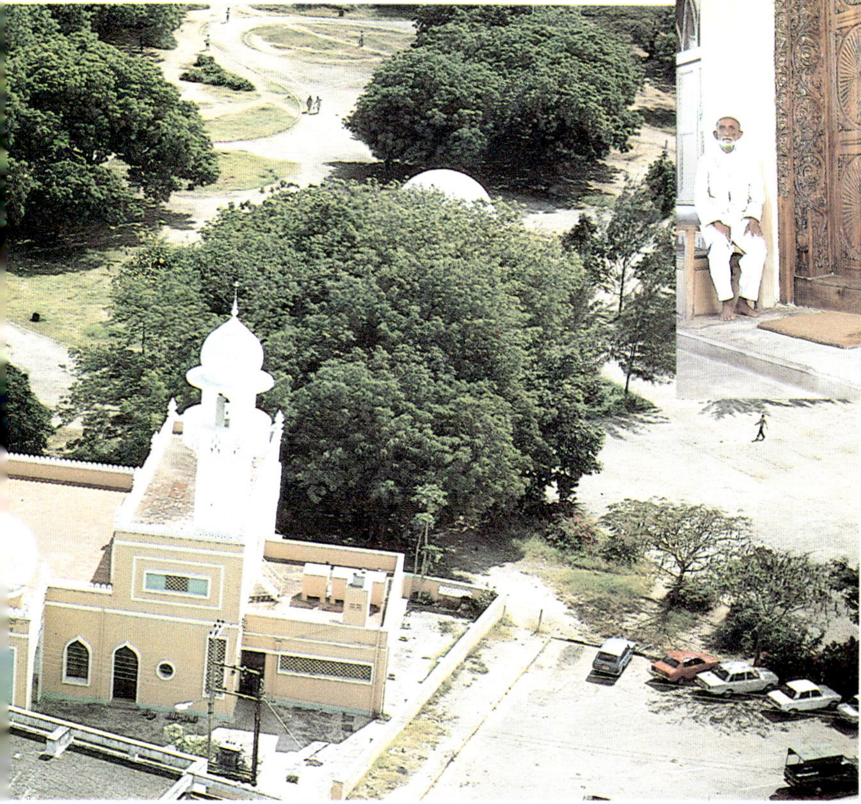

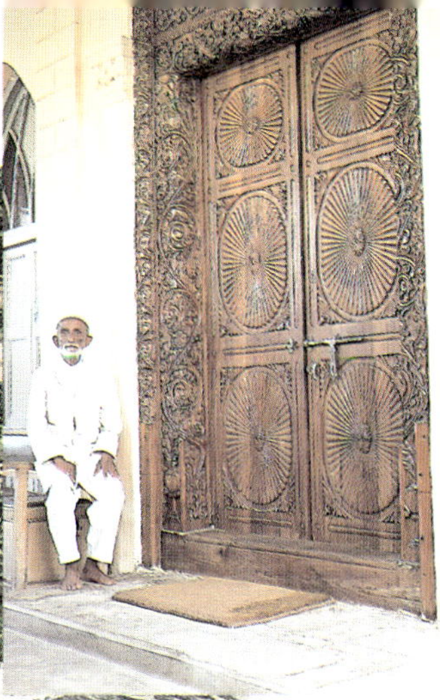

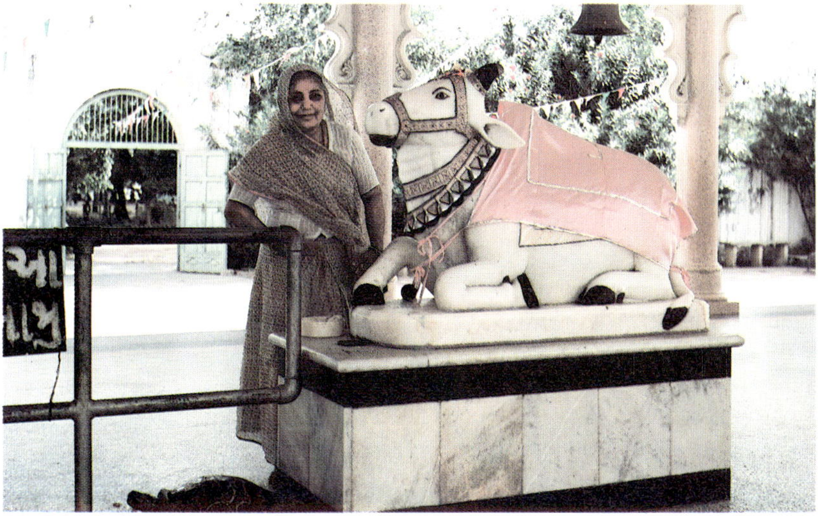

PLACES OF WORSHIP

The Holy Ghost Cathedral

The Catholic cathedral is in the centre of Mombasa at the junction of Nkrumah and Nyerere Avenues. It has a fine facade, with arched doors at the top of a wide stairway and twin Romanesque towers, but sadly it has been dwarfed by a recent high-rise block.

The cathedral was built mainly of coral blocks quarried from the space between the Manor Hotel and Ralli House, on the understanding that the Holy Ghost Fathers (the Cathedral's welfare is in the hands of the Irish Province of the Holy Ghost Fathers) constructed a road between it and the hotel. Nyerere Avenue owes its origin to this agreement.

The cathedral was completed in 1923. The impressive High Altar is of Italian marble and the richly coloured stained glass windows came from France and Ireland. An electric organ was installed in 1938. The land had belonged to the Catholics since 1891, however, bought by Father le Roy who arrived in Mombasa dressed as an Arab. His first church is now the bookshop adjoining the cathedral.

Mass is said in both English and Swahili – the latter service often accompanied by the beat of African drums.

Emmanuel Church, Freretown

This Anglican church is on your left as you pass through the tollgate leaving the Nyali Bridge, the building of which separated it from its bell-tower. This bell-tower is a feature of the junction between the Bamburi Road and the road that leads to Nyali and the area is known as Kengeleni, 'the place of the bell'.

Emmanuel Church is the second oldest in Kenya, the oldest being at Rabai. It was built in 1884 by freed slaves soon after their establishment in the Kisauni area, near a bell-tower erected by their settlement in 1875, on land given to the Church Missionary Society by the princes of Malindi in the early 1800s. Close by, around the Kisauni beach area, were the divinity school, the bishop's house, library and lady missionaries' house. (The first unmarried lady missionaries arrived in 1885.) All these buildings still stand but they are now private houses.

In 1878 Bishop Royston of Mauritius wrote to the CMS in London: 'The Great Bell – hourly struck, near the landing place and office, day and night, by one of the settlement's watchmen – loudly summoned us to the school and chapel...' The bell was rung hourly, day and night, as a warning to intending slave raiders. The bell in the church tower, dated 1896, is said to be the original made by John Warner and Sons, London. If this is so it was probably recast as the tower and bell were reconstructed some years before Emmanuel Church.

A covered arcade surrounds the church, and inside there is a high, semicircular arch over the approach to the choir. On it, the words *'Watamwita Jina Lakwe Imanueli Mngu Pamoja Naswi'* exhort the congregation to 'Call his name Emmanuel...' In the vestry hangs a picture of Matthew Wellington, one of the Africans sent in search of Livingstone whom they found near Ujiji, and whose embalmed body they presented to the British Consul at the Coast. Matthew was buried in the CMS graveyard near the church, amongst missionaries, sailors and government officials.

The church is well attended and plays an important role in the lives of the African Christian community.

Mosques

Mombasa's mosques are generally plain buildings with a large main hall. The room is undecorated and off it are ablution rooms where hands and feet can be washed before entering the main hall. The *qibla* (the recess facing Mecca) forms part of one wall; beside it there is often a *mimbar* from which the priest or imam makes announcements and reads prayers. In some sects there is no *mimbar* because of the belief that no man is more important than any other in the mosque and cannot stand higher than his fellows.

Mombasa Island has more than a hundred mosques in use. Architecturally, the most interesting ones are in the Old Town.

Mandhry Mosque is a landmark as you walk from the Fort to the Old Port, its white minaret constrasting with the dark timbers of the balconies overhanging the street close by. Across the road is an ancient well from which it draws its water supplies. Its minaret is not unlike that of the **Tangana Mosque** on Old Kilindini Road.

A new feature of the Old Port is the attractive **Burhani Bohra Mosque.** The old mosque was built in 1902 by Mr. M. Jivanjee over the site of a very much older mosque and its graveyard. Situated between the fish market and Leven steps, this new mosque, with its tall minaret and many added facilities, is an elegant addition to the architecture of the area.

One of the most imposing buildings in the Old Town is the Imami Ismaili **Jamat-khana** at Kuze, which dates from 1885. This is one of the mosques of the Aga Khan community. It has a handsome entrance door leading from the courtyard into a large communal hall and from upstairs to the north are views of the dhow careening area at Pwaa Kuu and the harbour beyond.

Close by, where Kuze Street meets Nehru Road, is the **Sindhi Memon Jamia.** Just down Samburu Road between Nehru and Old Kilindini Roads, is the **Bhadala Mosque** with a colourful dome and minaret. The Bhadalas were a seafaring people and among the first immigrants.

Outside the Old Town there are four mosques worthy of mention. The **Baluchi Mosque,** behind the main Post Office and on one side of the Jamhuri Gardens, belongs to the Baluchi community who first came to East Africa troops of the Imam of Muscat. Its dome and minaret are a welcome relief between the parking bays on either side.

Looking from the Post Office down Gusii Street, the **Sheikh Jundani Mosque** catches the eye with its curved dome and high minaret. It stands on the site of an older mosque built in 1870 of mud and wattle by a community of water carriers from the Hadhramaut. It was rebuilt in 1958 from funds made available by the Busaidi family. In the grounds near the mosque are the graves of Salim bin Khalfan and his sons Ali bin Salim and Seif bin Salim. In a room open to one side and opposite the *qibla* is the tomb of Sheikh Jundani, a revered saint.

The **Yusufi Mosque** at the Polytechnic, with its emerald green dome, forms part of the attractive Arabic architecture of this complex and is one of the few non-denominational mosques.

If you go into a mosque, be sure to remove your shoes at the entrance. Nearly all the mosques exclude women.

Hindu temples

The Jain Temple
This temple is off Langoni Road and is reached through a covered passageway in the buildings of the Jain Community Centre. Once in the courtyard, a strikingly beautiful white edifice meets your eye. The temple is made from marble imported from India; the architect and the artisans were also imported because of their experience in building temples in Kathiawar. The roof consists of rounded domes, pyramids and a cluster of towers, the tallest of which is in the centre. It is supported by stout pillars

between whose capitals are curving arches, some of a ropelike appearance.

Inside, opposite the entrance, the main hall is dominated by a small recess with three statues of the Lords of Jainism. Lord Mahavir is the dominant, central figure. The hall is beautifully decorated with relief sculpture and painted scenes of ancient temples.

Lord Shiva's Temple

The temple is at one side of the open parking space adjacent to Jamhuri Gardens. Its tall spire topped by a bust of Lord Shiva, a pot of gold above his head, once dwarfed all the other buildings on the Island. It was built in 1955 by the Hindu Union and new additions will soon be completed on Mwagogo Road.

Inside the main gate are spacious grounds around the temple which are always full of pigeons. A large covered area leads up

The green-tiled dome of Yusufi Mosque, and the Polytechnic

to the main sanctuary and this is used by both men and women for study meetings.

On a pedestal at one end, gazing into the sanctuary, lies the sacred bull, Lord Shiva's guard, below which is a tortoise, symbol of purity. Between here and the sanctuary, which is at a lower level, is a magnificent six-panelled silver door. The top two panels show the sun god in his chariot and the moon god in a simple chariot drawn by a deer. The central panels depict Lord Shiva dancing with his partner Parvati. On the bottom panel are Lord Shiva's family and 'Aum', representing the first sound uttered at creation. On either side of the door are Shiva's elephant-headed son, Ganapati, and Hanuman, the monkey god.

Inside the sanctuary the Sacred Cobra, usually bedecked with flowers and leaves, lies coiled on the Shiva Linga, a holy object brought from India. Lord Shiva's statue is on one wall.

The Shree Cutch Satang Swami Narayan Temple

Situated on Haile Selassie Road, this is an exceedingly ornate temple and attracts many visitors with its bright paintwork and carvings. The building is topped by a colourful tower on the four faces of which are large relief paintings. The one facing the street shows Krishna and his adoring cows; in the other paintings are Laxmi, goddess of finance; Saraswatti, goddess of education and the arts, and Druv, who as a child was cast out by his family and endured hardship in the jungle.

In niches on either side of the vast entrance door stand figures of two guards. Above the door is a relief painting of Lord Krishna and his companion, Radha. Two cows listen attentively to the flute he is playing. The twelve-panelled door depicts the reincarnations of Krishna whose head, neck, body and legs form eight curves – the *ashta*.

Inside are two main prayer halls, one above the other. Women use the ground floor, men the upper. At one end of the men's hall are large relief pictures, with the Swami in pride of place in the centre. To the left, the Swami is shown with Lord Krishna and Radha; to the right are the earthly and heavenly representations of Krishna.

8. Mainland North

Nyali Bridge

The crossing from Mombasa Island to Mainland North used to be by small rowing boats. One started from the beach just upcreek from the Island end of the Nyali Pontoon Bridge and crossed to Kisauni beach; another went from the Old Port to English Point. Nyali Pontoon Bridge, dating from 1931 and one of the world's longest pontoon bridges, took over and served well. The new bridge, which crosses the creek from Buxton to Ras Kisauni, has now been completed and you may not be aware of the history of the old Nyali bridge which no longer exists. The new bridge forms a continuation of Ronald Ngala Road on the mainland and once over it the road continues as the Bamburi Road.

Nyali Bridge was originally built and put in position by Nyali Ltd, a company who had bought a large sisal estate with a view to converting it into an attractive residential area. The bridge was necessary to enable residents to travel to and from work on the Island. Over the years buildings extended inland from the sea front, mainly in plots of about 5 hectares (2 acres). The area is now Mombasa's exclusively developed garden suburb, with large villas and luxuriant gardens.

Kisauni and Freretown

Kisauni and Freretown encompass the main road north after crossing the new bridge and form a considerable area to the left of the road. Historically they were greatly involved in accommodating and protecting freed slaves; the Church Missionary Society played a major role in looking after Africans who had been taken into slavery in Nyasaland (Malawi) and areas to its north and east. Slaves rescued from the dhows were mostly brought to Kisauni. The settlement was started in 1874 and in the latter part of the nineteenth century Emmanuel Church was built by freed slaves. Freretown was named after Sir Bartle Frere through whose good offices much was done for the slaves. Near the church

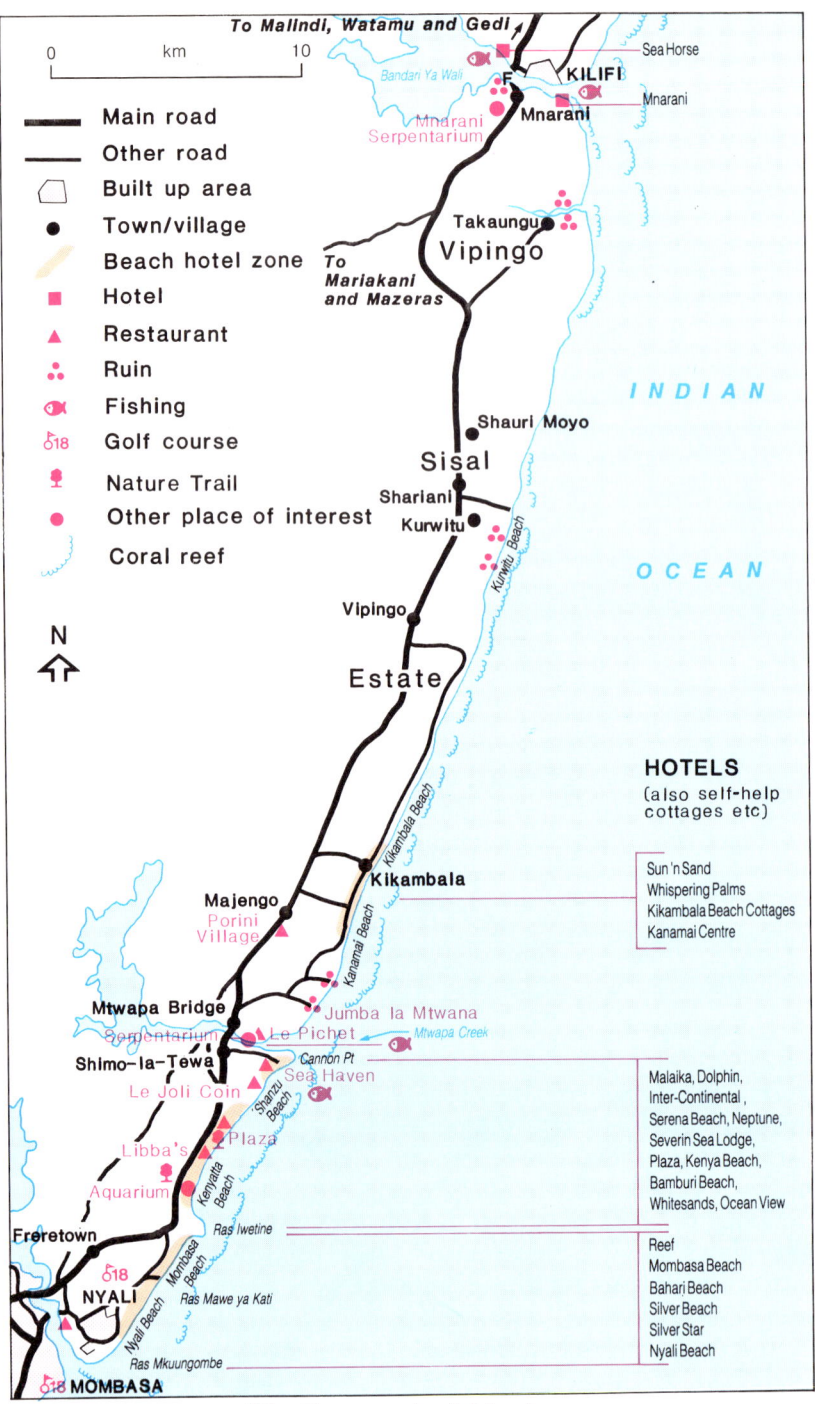

The Coast north of Mombasa

is the Bacchus supermarket complex.

Looking down the creek from the new bridge towards the Old Harbour the boats of the **Bahari Club** can be seen sheltering off Kisauni beach. The Old Town stands out, beyond a promontory to the right, below which boats are repaired. To the left is the **Tamarind Restaurant,** a popular place for lunch and dinner. Further on, past some flats, the cement silos at English Point are a landmark. Beyond them are the remains of the **Mombasa Marina** and behind the marina, on a small hill, is the **Krapf Memorial** – a tall cross rising from a cubical base on whose four sides are panels in Swahili and English describing Krapf's ministry and travels. Krapf was a CMS Missionary and wrote the first Swahili dictionary. He died in 1881. He and a fellow missionary, Rebmann, were the first Europeans to see the awe-inspiring views of the snow-capped mountains, Kilimanjaro and Kenya. Next to the memorial is the **Agricultural Society's showground.** The annual Show is at the end of August.

The beaches

North of the entrance to the Old Harbour as far as Malindi stretch superb beaches of fine, clean, white coral sand, separated by headlands and creeks. A coral reef, at varying distances from the shore, keeps out the larger predator fishes so bathing is safe along both north and south coasts. Visits to the reef at low tide are popular; so too are trips in glass-bottomed boats.

The first beach is backed by Nyali Estate and ends at Ras Mkuungombe. Next is **Nyali Beach,** also backed by the Estate, with the **Nyali Beach Hotel,** the oldest beach hotel in Kenya. Further north Ras Mawe ya Kati separates Nyali Beach from **Mombasa Beach,** overlooked by **Mombasa Beach Hotel** which has a plastic water slide, said to be the longest in the world. It starts its curving course some 30 metres above a small swimming pool on the beach, where the slide ends. Above the promontory are the **Silver Beach** and **Bahari Beach Hotels.** The estate behind this beach is relatively new and is called **Mji Mpya,** or 'New Town'. The **Reef Hotel** is near the northern end of this beach. Another headland, Ras Iwetine, separates Mombasa Beach from **Kenyatta Beach.** There are many smaller hotels along this stretch – the largest being **Bamburi Beach, Severin Sea Lodge, Plaza, Neptune** and **Whitesand.**

In Mombasa
we're the Five Star hotel by which
all others are measured.

HOTEL
INTER•CONTINENTAL
MOMBASA

THE ADVANTAGE IS INTER•CONTINENTAL®

INTER•CONTINENTAL HOTELS

Shanzur P.O. Box 83492, Telex: 21153 Telephone: 485811

Le Joli Coin and **Libba's Restaurant** are two excellent places to go for a meal, especially dinner. At **Severin Sea Lodge** a local dhow has been hauled up near the hotel front and has been converted into the **Dhow Restaurant.** The sound of the waves breaking on the beach immediately below you adds a romantic touch to the evening. This beach is separated by another headland from **Shanzu Beach** where there are several good hotels: **Coral Beach, Dolphin, Malaika** and the **New Inter-Continental.** The most striking hotel here is the **Serena,** built to simulate typical Lamu or Shela houses. There are plenty of *ngalawas* (dug-out canoes with outriggers either side) here to take you to the reef. Windsurfing is also popular.

Nyali Bridge to Mtwapa Bridge

Starting from the new Nyali Bridge and travelling straight on past the Nyali turning, the main road north takes you to Mtwapa Bridge. On your left after leaving the village of Freretown is the Bamburi Cement Factory. You see it first across a desert of bare yellow sand and then a green woodland emerges where the Company is making a successful attempt to reclaim the desert-like area from which the coral has been quarried. The agronomist, René Haller, has planted a variety of trees, made a lake and is breeding tilapia fish commercially. He has populated the area with a number of animals and at feeding time the young hippo, water buck, oryx, and some small duiker appear as if by magic at the lake. There is a variey of birdlife here too: the sacred ibis stealing the show from the Egyptian geese and others. The reclamation area is reached by taking the road to the left which goes to the Cement Company, where a Nature Trail starts. Further along the main road on the seaward side near the Severin Sea Lodge you will see notices to another nature trail also designed by René Haller. It would be wise to enquire when it is open to the public before making the trip. The telephone number is 485501.

Turning right off the Bamburi Road, immediately opposite the Cement Company road, signs point to the **Aquarium.** This is attractively set out with large tanks showing different varieties of fish, many of them very colourful; there is also the dangerous stonefish. Other tanks contain beautiful coral heads and there is a fascinating variety of crustaceans. Jacques Allard, who constructed the aquarium, will talk to visitors about his collection.

Car Hire
Excursions
Safaris
Hotel/Lodge Bookings
Air Travel

Contact Frances Cook

Flamingo Tours
(Coast) Limited

P.O. Box 83321
Telephone: 311978/9
Telex 21061
Mombasa
Kenya

Terrace Floor, Ambalal House

Above: Serena Beach Hotel, resembling Lamu architecture

Right: Sally the Hippo at Bamburi Nature Trail

Left: Giriama dancers with swirling skirts, performing in the grounds of a Coastal hotel

MAINLAND NORTH

NATURE TRAIL

BAMBURI NATURE TRAIL

The major requisite in the manufacture of cement is limestone. For a million years or more living coral polyps have lived in congregation in the shore waters of the Indian Ocean and, in dying left a concretion of limestone that formed the reef barrier of the Bamburi coastline, just north of Mombasa, Kenya. These ancient reefs provide the basis for Baobab cement.

The Bamburi Cement Company over the past thirty years has used an open cast mining system covering a large area of the countryside. In depth the mining stops just above the water table, at sea level. The process has left a desert which was becoming a conservationists' nightmare.

In 1971 the cement company with an eye for conservation and ecological balance laid out a 35 ha. experimental plot. Today that project is known as "**THE BAMBURI NATURE TRAIL**".

Over the years the formidable and bare landscape has changed as though with a touch of a magic wand. Where once the sun scorched the rock now one finds forest, glade, ponds and streams. The trees provide shade to the creatures that thrive on the evergreen vegetation. Twenty five metres high, the trees cast shadows over the waters of ponds that team with the fish, **Tilapia**. In the glades wild animals roam. And all this happens no more than a stones throw from the hotels and crowded tropical beaches of Bamburi.

The rehabilitation of the quarry began with the excavation of fish ponds and trials of different species of trees. The fish ponds soon turned into a commercial fish farm. Reafforestation, too was successful even under extreme and harsh conditions. Tree planting necessitated the digging of a hole to establish each seedling in the rock floor of the quarry. Then came the introduction of other flora and fauna to create a balanced ecosystem teaming with wildlife, a **MINI SAFARI PARK** and Game Sanctuary.

The result is a wildlife paradise, a birdwatcher's dream and a botanist's delight. Here can be seen the magnificent eland, oryx, waterbuck, warthog, bush pig, crocodile, monkeys and last but not least the Nature Trails mascot, Sally, the baby hippo who has been at Bamburi since 1975.

So if you are a visitor to the coast you do not have to go far to see wildlife in a natural setting. Bamburi Quarry Nature Trail is known by conservationists all over the world as a living experiment of wasteland rehabilitation; a microcosm of a continent's age old beauty where flora and fauna live together in great content. Come see for yourself.

Continuing along the Malindi road, turnings to the right lead to hotels and private houses and later to the Shanzu beach. On the left, almost opposite the turning to the Sagar Restaurant, is a road leading to the **Sea Haven Restaurant,** which has been taken over by the **African Safari Club.** It caters for almost every variety of water sports.

If you prefer, instead of using the main road, you can take the old road to the left, just before reaching a new mosque, that runs through coconut plantations and African villages and rejoins the main road past the Sea Haven Restaurant. On the way, you pass another new mosque.

Travelling further along the north-bound road you reach Mtwapa Bridge which crosses Mtwapa Creek, Mombasa's municipal boundary. **Shimo-la-Tewa** prison and secondary school are on either side of the road as you approach the bridge. Shimo-la-Tewa means 'the hole or cave of the rock cod'.

For those interested in deep-sea fishing there are two experienced fishing establishments on the northern side of the Creek and **Le Pichet Restaurant** provides an excellent cuisine. Near the restaurant is a marina, **Kenya Marineland** and **Serpentarium,** with an aquarium and snake park. Some of the larger fishes are displayed here, and you can watch them being fed and observe their underwater activities through windows at different depths.

A Samburu village is close at hand, where visitors are welcome.

Instead of carrying straight on after crossing the Nyali Bridge, you can turn right towards Nyali and follow the notices to the Crocodile Farm, called **Mamba Village,** opposite the Nyali Golf and County Club on Links Road. It has been built in an old lime quarry, and the crocodiles, which range from small young ones up to full-grown males, live in man-made pools linked by small canals. The thatched pagoda-style building which houses the bar and restaurant may be used separately or one may wish to pay the entrance fee to the viewing area and enjoy a guided tour plus explanatory video. Either way it is a pleasant place to sit over a drink or meal, especially at night with the lights shining over the garden and pools.

The Jumba Ruins and Takaungu

About 2 kilometres (1.25 miles) north of Mtwapa Bridge is a

turning to **Jumba la Mtwana** which has been properly cleared and studied only in the last ten years. This is the remains of a slave-trading settlement (Jumba la Mtwana means 'the house of the slave') dating from the fourteenth or fifteenth century. The township covers an area a little smaller than Gedi, a walled Arab township near Malindi which was destroyed in the seventeenth century. It has the mosque and tomb ruins typical of the East African Coast and houses with interesting arched doorways. How the area came to be deserted is not known. The buildings extend down to a pleasant beach where you can picnic and bathe.

Nearly 1 kilometre (just over half a mile) further along the main road from the Jumba turning is the **Porini Village Restaurant** which serves local African dishes and puts on displays of African dancing. A little after that a turning to the right leads to **Whispering Palms Hotel** and the **Kikambala Beach Cottages.** Whispering Palms has a distinctive architecture with high *makuti* (palm leaf thatch) roofing, and the beach here is good for bathing. Not far beyond this turning is another to **Sun'N Sand**, a pleasant hotel on the same beach. If you are feeling energetic you may prefer to walk the 2-kilometre track along the Coast through the coconut groves from the Kanamai Conference and Holiday Centre to this beach.

The road leads on past small farms and villages through the large **Vipingo Sisal Estate.** Sisal was first grown here in 1934 and the Estate, with its factories, workers' housing and narrow-gauge railway, now covers an area of about 50 000 hectares (over 20 000 acres). A turn to the right leads to beach houses at Vipingo and Kurwitu. The beach here is broken up into several small private areas by coral headlands.

For a short length the main road is enveloped by cashew nut trees and some coconut palms. The village of Shariani and its school nestle among the trees. Beyond Shariani the sisal plantation again comes down to the road. Striking companions to the sisal are the weird baobab trees; they seem to have smoother trunks than those in Mombasa and appear to know no season; you may see a leafless tree beside another covered with leaves and fruit.

Where the Sisal Estate ends is the village of **Takaunga,** a place of considerable importance during the Mazrui period. As in many places along the Coast there are old ruins here, both on the northern and southern banks of the small creek. Takaungu has several haunted houses and quite phlegmatic and stable people

Jumba la Mtwana ruins near Mtwapa

who have stayed a night in one of these tell of seeing and being aware of ghosts in the house, while outside there was an eerie sound of the clanking of slave chains.

It was at Takaungu that a revolt against the administration of the Imperial British East Africa Company started over the selection of a new *liwali* (local governor), following the death of the previous incumbent. The Mazruis thought that the British had chosen wrongly and insisted on another with greater rights. Plantations were burnt and attacks made on the Company's property. The revolt was soon put down, but Mbaruk, the instigator, escaped and took up residence in Gazi well to the south of Mombasa.

There is an attractive beach at Takaungu which can be reached by driving through the village.

Kilifi and Mnarani

Beyond Takaungu is undulating countryside covered by smallholdings of maize. Towards Kilifi these give way to large open fields with a few trees and some fine cattle. These belong to **Kilifi Plantations.** The township is mainly on the northern side of the creek and the village and farms on the southern side form the district of **Mnarani** (which means 'the place of the minaret or tower'). This area was important during Portuguese days and is frequently mentioned in their writings.

The main road leads down to the ferry crossing. On your left as you go down the hill is a pathway to the old ruins of Mnarani and the **serpentarium** which is housed in a large *makuti*-thatched house. The ruins are well worth a visit. Follow the path and climb the many steps leading through a coral outcrop to the level ground above. The site has not been completely cleared but there are interesting tombs, one with a high pillar, and two ruined mosques. A bonus is the superb view of the creek and the ferry plying across the water.

The people of Mnarani came under attack from the Galla and were virtually wiped out. James Kirkman, who has done a great deal of historical research on the Coast, believes that the inhabitants locked themselves into the main mosque. Maybe it was the Galla who caused the desertion of Jumba and Gedi.

The **Mnarani Hotel,** which used to be the Mnarani Club, is one of the most popular deep-sea fishing sites along the Coast. Built on a high coral bluff, it commands wonderful views both towards the entrance to the creek and inland. There is excellent anchorage near the mouth of the creek and large sailing ships and motor boats make a colourful scene. Wind surfing and water skiing can be enjoyed or you may like to sail up the creek to where the waterway opens out. Carmine bee eaters nest on the small islands and at this time the islands take on a crimson hue as dusk approaches.

The main town and *boma* are on the northern side of the creek, including the administrative centre, hospital and cashew nut factory. Up-creek from the ferry there is a good beach, and here the **Sea Horse Hotel** provides good food and facilities, and fine views.

9. South Coast

The Kenya Bus Company runs the Likoni Ferry from Mombasa Island to Likoni. As you cross, look up the harbour towards the **Yatch Club** and the ships beyond lying alongside the jetties or anchored in the stream. Across the harbour is **Peleleza,** Sir Ali bin Salim's old home, and beyond it the Naval headquarters.

Reaching the other side you drive up the steep slope of the ferry approach, through Likoni, to the main road leading to the South Coast beaches and hotels.

The beaches and coral reefs

Turn left at the top of the slope from the ferry and you pass through a residential area to reach the **Shelly Beach Hotel.** The road commands good views of the Island and Mainland North. The Andromache Reef surrounds this corner of the Coast, extending a protecting arm across the seaward side of the Island. The beach is indeed shelly and low tide reveals a considerable area of coral and fascinating pools. You can walk out on the reef (plastic sandals are advised) and may be tempted to bathe in one of the deeper pools. Watch out for the spiky sea urchin!

Travelling along the main road past Likoni you pass many cashew-nut trees, interspersed with coconut palms and larger kapok trees whose fruit bursts to expose the kapok inside (this, of course, is the kapok used for filling pillows and mattresses). Large mango trees provide shade on the roadside.

After the villages of Ngombeni and Waa there is a large coconut plantation. The turning to **Kwale** is just before the end of the plantation, 17 kilometres (about 10.5 miles) from Likoni. The attractive administrative centre and the **Shimba Hills National Park** are described at the end of this chapter. Continuing on the main road you soon come to a turning on the left with signs to Maweni Cottages, Capricho, Moonlight Bay and Sand Island Cottages. Further on is a turning to **Twiga Beach Hotel,** Twigalets and several residential plots. The road is a horseshoe – you eventually emerge on the main road again.

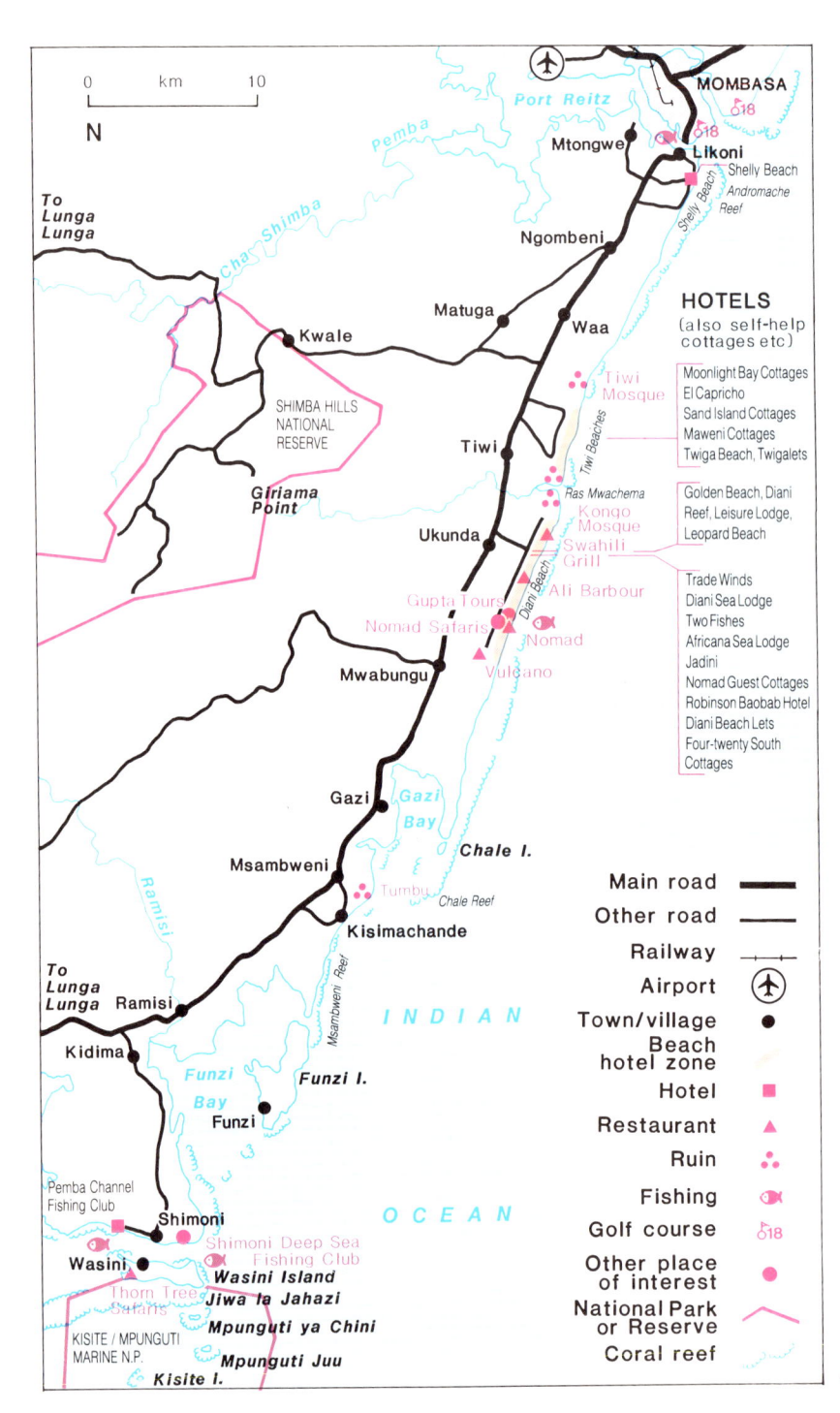

The Coast south of Mombasa

HOTELS (also self-help cottages etc)

Moonlight Bay Cottages
El Capricho
Sand Island Cottages
Maweni Cottages
Twiga Beach, Twigalets

Golden Beach, Diani Reef, Leisure Lodge, Leopard Beach

Trade Winds
Diani Sea Lodge
Two Fishes
Africana Sea Lodge
Jadini
Nomad Guest Cottages
Robinson Baobab Hotel
Diani Beach Lets
Four-twenty South Cottages

Legend:
- Main road
- Other road
- Railway
- Airport
- Town/village
- Beach hotel zone
- Hotel
- Restaurant
- Ruin
- Fishing
- Golf course
- Other place of interest
- National Park or Reserve
- Coral reef

Places labelled on map: Mombasa, Mtongwe, Likoni, Shelly Beach, Andromache Reef, Port Reitz, Pemba, To Lunga Lunga, Ngombeni, Cha Shimba, Matuga, Kwale, Waa, Tiwi Mosque, Shimba Hills National Reserve, Tiwi, Tiwi Beaches, Giriama Point, Ras Mwachema, Ukunda, Kongo Mosque, Swahili Grill, Gupta Tours, Ali Barbour, Nomad Safaris, Diani Beach, Nomad, Mwabungu, Vulcano, Gazi, Gazi Bay, Chale I., Msambweni, Tumbu, Chale Reef, Kisimachande, Ramisi, To Lunga Lunga, Kidima, Msambweni Reef, Funzi Bay, Funzi I., Funzi, Pemba Channel Fishing Club, Shimoni, Shimoni Deep Sea Fishing Club, Wasini, Wasini Island, Jiwa la Jahazi, Thorn Tree Safaris, Kisite/Mpunguti Marine N.P., Mpunguti ya Chini, Mpunguti Juu, Kisite I.

Indian Ocean

SOUTH COAST

Above: Diani beach, glimpsed through coconut palms and flamboyants

Leopard Beach Hotel at the northern end of Diani beach

67

This stretch of seafront is divided into many small, attractive beaches by coral outcrops and the reef is quite close. In places there are sandy areas which make it easier to reach the reef, and at **Sand Island** there is a permanent, though moving, island of sand. The water here is very clear and goggling is excellent. There are scattered sites with old ruins, but none of them seems to be large enough to call a village or town.

Back on the main road you continue south over a small bridge which spans the Tiwi River. The river varies considerably in size and at times during the dry season it may be almost dry. The road continues to Ukunda.

The large turning to the left goes to **Diani Beach** and the many hotels and houses along its length. This is probably the best stretch of sand in East Africa; the reef is about half a mile off shore, and at mid-tide the variety of blues and greens in the water is magnificent. The road runs parallel to the beach which for much of its length has waving coconut palms and casuarina trees forming a backcloth to this attractive tropical scene.

Opposite each of the main hotel areas African *ngalawas* anchor amongst the motor boats and occasional sailing boat. At low tide it is great fun to hire one of these to sail to the reef, where you can swim on the sandy landward side and investigate the many pools, each with a variety of fish, crabs, coral heads and other fascinating living creatures.

Nomad Safaris, just south of **Jadini Hotel,** arrange trips to **Chale Island** further down the Coast. On the way the boat drops anchor for about half an hour for a goggling session. Then you are landed on the beach at Chale Island to swim, sunbathe or explore the small coral island while an excellent lunch is cooked. After lunch, the boats return to base. Nomad also arrange deep-sea fishing trips.

Gupta Tours also arrange deep-sea fishing trips and their local office is opposite the entrance to the Jadini Hotel.

Another popular pastime, usually during the northern monsoon, is to float suspended from a large, colourful parachute, drawn along by a Land Rover on the beach. The organizers have a team who see to it that you have no problems at take-off or landing.

Most of the hotels have first-class swimming pools and at Leopard Beach there is a casino for those with money to risk. The hotels on the beach can be seen on the maps. The northernmost part of this beach reaches as far as the mouth of the Tiwi River.

There is an old mosque ruin, recently partly restored, known as the **Kongo Mosque.** The pillars are the length of a *boriti* (mangrove) pole apart: the roofing was made of these poles plastered over with coral rag. It has several domes and must have been impressive in its day. There are some old ruins on the northern bank of the Tiwi, but these are difficult to get to and perhaps not worth seeking out. If you do go, take the precaution of having a friend with you because the occasional robbery is not unknown. The beach is good here and the bathing quite safe.

At the other end of Diani Beach, past the prominence on which the Robinson Baobab stands, the beach is coral at first, with two beach-cottage establishments – Four-twenty South and Beach Lets – where it becomes sandy again. In this area there is a small shipyard building *ngalawas*. It is planned to build more hotels further south where there are attractive beaches.

An Italian restaurant, **Vulcanos,** with very smart decor, provides high class Italian dishes. Mention should also be made of the **Ali Barbour Restaurant,** very cleverly built into natural coral caves. The decor is coastal with many Lamu-type carved tables and doors. The management have built a beach bar on the sea-front where snacks are served.

A goggling session with Nomad Safaris

Gazi village

Back again at Ukunda Village you can continue south on the main Lunga Lunga road. At the 36-kilometre (22.25 mile) mark you pass through the small village of Mwabungu; on either side is a plantation of cashew-nut trees. Further on is a coconut plantation and a copra-processing factory. At about the 40-kilometre (25 mile) mark take the left turn for Gazi, a village close to the sea at Maftaha or **Gazi Bay.** Gazi is of historical interest for during the Mazrui revolt against the British East Africa Company in 1895, Sheikh Mbaruk bin Rashid Al Mazrui led the southern section of the family and set up his headquarters here. Plantations were destroyed by fire and attacks made on other villages. The British sent troops to quell the revolt, but Mbaruk escaped to German East Africa.

Mbaruk's large house, with its magnificent 'Arab' door, still stands in the village, although the top storey has been removed. The floor is covered by layers of legal papers, having once been a *mudir's* court. Few people dare to enter the room for grizzly tales are told about the house. One such is that there was a superstition that if a human body was buried in the foundations the house would be stronger and last longer. Eight men and eight women were decapitated and buried in lines in the foundations. Two rooms on the ground floor have a corner filled in by a large conical projection, said to contain several bodies.

Mbaruk's aide had a reputation for murder almost worse than his master's. His room in the house is said to be visited once a week by a group of women who burn incense to appease his spirit.

Some people claim that, while returning home from evening prayers, they see a group of Arabs in a circle round a fire near the house. When they look back after passing them no one is there and there is no fire. It is said that no dog or donkey can live in the village. If one strays in it will die mysteriously after a very short time.

The beach is not far away, but a walk through mangrove swamps to reach it will discourage all but enthusiasts.

Msambweni and Ramisi

At roughly the 48-kilometre (30 mile) mark along the main road you come to the important village and government centre of Msambweni, 'place of the sable antelope', which lies almost entirely between the main road and the sea. On the inland side of the road is the start of the large Ramisi Sugar Estate.

If you turn left off the main road and continue through the village past the Police Barracks you come to the Government Hospital, and about 2 kilometres (1.25 miles) up the beach to the north there is an old walled ruin known as **Tumbe.** It is quite large and has only one doorway which is situated on the southern aspect. It is believed that this was a holding place for slaves. Attractive new houses have recently been built close to the beach north of the hospital and more are under construction.

Between Msambweni and Ramisi, an area of 4455 hectares (11000 acres) grows six varieties of sugar cane. The main sugar factory, which belongs to the Associated Sugar Company, is at Ramisi itself, a township founded in 1927, some 16 kilometres (about 10 miles) from Msambweni. The land to your right from Ukunda to Ramisi is remarkably flat, and fresh water is never very far below the surface. There is a theory that rivulets starting on the slopes of Mount Kilimanjaro take an underground course at

A male Agama lizard, frequently seen at the Coast

the foot of the mountain, and after running under the Usambara Mountains form a vast pool just below the surface in this area. Whatever the cause, sugar benefits from this bountiful water supply.

Ramisi is near the edge of **Funzi Bay.** The old villages of Shirazi and Bodo nestle close to the islands and mangroves of the bay. Funzi Island itself forms the seaward boundary of the bay.

Continuing along the main road the country soon changes to gentle green hills and *doum* palms. The Tanzania border is across lusher valleys at Lunga Lunga.

Shimoni and Pemba Channel

Just after Ramisi you turn off the road for Shimoni and the **Pemba Channel Fishing Club,** passing through the little village of Kidima on the way.

Shimoni is a fishing village, delightfully situated at the southern end of a broad, almost square peninsula, south of Ramisi. 'Shimoni' means 'the place of the hole': there is a large opening near the end of the main road where you turn off to the Fishing Club. Inside the hole tunnels lead off in several directions, the height varying between 1 and 10 metres.

Some 50 metres (about 45 yards) away is another quite sizeable opening. In places a small rock has been placed over a hole for safety. If you remove the rock and drop a small stone into the hole you realize how deep the cavity is. It is as if most of the area stood on an eggshell, with supporting sponge-like struts. Some years ago an army patrol investigating the length of the 'tunnel' walked inland for over 11 kilometres (7 miles). It is recorded that slavers lowered captured Africans into the cave and marched them to Shimoni where dhows awaited them.

The old District Commissioner's house still stands, but it is roofless and slowly breaking up. It looks an imposing building now and must have been an impressive house seventy or more year ago. Close by is the well-kept grave of Captain Lawrence who was killed in the Mazrui rebellion.

From Shimoni you can look across Wasini Channel to the Island of Wasini. Up and down the Channel *ngalawas, mitumbwi* (dug out canoes), small *jahazis* and motorized fishing boats of the Pemba Channel Fishing Club ply to and fro. The Club is about 1 kilometre (just over half a mile) from the end of the main road at Shimoni. It has a fine fishing record and the bandas (self-help bungalows) are usually fully booked during the fishing season, such is its reputation. For those who remain ashore there is a swimming pool and other amenities. The owners at the time of writing have developed the art of coping with irregularly returning boats and hungry landlubbers, with remarkable culinary skill.

Wasini Island

Wasini Island, a narrow strip of land lying east-west in its axis, is across the water from Shimoni. It is about 3 kilometres (nearly 2 miles) long and 1 kilometre (just over half a mile) across. There are two villages on the island: Wasini, facing Shimoni, and Mkwiro at the eastern end which is much more recent in origin.

The name 'Wasini' perhaps derives from the Swahili words *wasi wasi*, meaning doubt, uncertainty or disquiet, so Wasini may mean 'a place of uncertainty'. Some call it the Forgotten Island. The first known inhabitants were the Wavumba, a community from Vumba Kuu. Old people say that Vumba, which is on the mainland near the present Tanzanian border, was repeatedly attacked by the Maasai. So its inhabitants moved south to Kigomeni, a short distance south of the present border. This place was short of fresh water, so they moved again this time to Wasini. Here they found the remains of a water tank, but no other evidence of previous occupation. They cleared the bush and gradually houses and mosques were built. The first mosque was built by Shariff Hassan bin Abubakar and bears the date 1126 AH, showing that the move occurred about 250 years ago. The grave of Hassan's father, Shariff Abubakar bin Sheikh, is near the waterfront, blue porcelain plates decorating its sides. A huge baobab tree growing through a surrounding wall shades one of the founders of Wasini, for these two Shariffs were the first people to come to live on the island.

Wasini unfortunately proved to have the same fresh-water problems as Kigomeni: wells dug to 3 metres (about 10 feet) produced only salt water. A large catchment area in the centre of the island is said to be capable of holding enough water to supply Wasini for a year, but it is usually dry. So most of the community moved to the mainland for work. Mkwiro was settled much later by fishermen from the Coast to the north of Shimoni: Funzi Island, Shirazi, Gazi and Msambweni. They have one mosque to Wasini's five. Wasini is the only place in East Africa with a

A fun trip from Nomads to the beach off Chale Island

wild goat population. They multiply under forbidding circumstances.

Wasini is thought by some to have been closely associated with the slave trade, but this seems unlikely since there was no special building on the island to accommodate slaves, and it is more likely that once loaded at Shimoni they were taken direct to the Zanzibar slave market.

Legend has it that a small dhow with several *Mashariffu* (descendants of the Prophet) on board ran aground off the southern side of the island. The dhow was turned to stone as *Jiwe la Jahazi* (jiwe means stone or rock). The Mashariffu were turned into white egrets that still fly around the site of the wreck.

On the Shimoni side of the island there is an impressive *makuti*-roofed restaurant where **Thorn Tree Safaris** bring their customers for a special seafood meal after taking them in a small dhow around the eastern end of the island and stopping at **Kisite Island** for a goggling session. The goggling at Kisite must be the best in East Africa. Passing the eastern end of Wasini on the way to Kisite Island you will probably pass between two coral islands, Mpunguti ya Chini and Mpunguti ya Juu. This is an area of underwater coral outcrops and shallows and a pilot who knows his way around is essential. Kisite is a small, mushroom-shaped coral outcrop which is almost covered at high tide.

SOUTH COAST

Kwale and the Shimba Hills

The turning to Kwale is about 17 kilometres (10.5 miles) from Likoni, before you reach the end of the coconut plantation. The distance on to Kwale is 16 kilometres (nearly 10 miles). The village itself is 380 metres (1,250 feet) above sea level and you pass through rolling countryside as you gradually make the ascent.

Above: A Tsavo elephant with the background of Chyulu Hills

A young situtunga

The cashew-nut trees at the side of the road give way to open country with wide vistas of the valleys and slopes of the Shimba Hills. The last part of the road ascends steeply to the Kwale Administrative District; the houses and government offices are scattered through an attractive wooded setting. As you leave the village the road curves to the left and a short run brings you to the entrance of the **Shimba Hills National Park.** If, instead of going left out of Kwale, you go down one of the smaller roads, straight on or to the right, you will be rewarded by magnificent views of **Port Reitz Creek** and Mombasa. Until thirty or more years ago the main Mombasa water supply came from here; the Shimba River runs down to an arm of Port Reitz Creek over to your left.

From the entrance to the Shimba Hills National Park the road continues to Lunga Lunga and eventually to Tanga. It used to be the main coast road to Tanzania. The Park is one of the few remaining places in Kenya where you can still see the beautiful sable antelope. They and the roan antelope breed well and there are several herds in the Park.

Near the centre of the Park is a thick forest – the Lango-Magandi Forest – and adjoining it is the airstrip. Roads radiate from the central forest and other roads cross these to enable you to get nearer the animals which interest you most. Going seawards you come to **Giriama Point,** the end of this particular road, from which there is a magnificent view of the coast overlooking the smaller hills and villages below. This is a good picnic area.

Approaching Giriama Point, roads to the right lead to **Sheldrick Falls** where you may see buffalo and even elephant. The elephants' main stronghold seems to be the central forest, but they often stray. When they have young, or when rain has brought a lushness to the foliage elsewhere, their droppings can be seen all over the Park.

There is another forest, the Makadara Forest, on the opposite side of the Park to the entrance gate. Continuing on this road you eventually reach the coast road again at Ramisi. The Park is small, so if you fail to see game in one area try adjacent areas or those opposite to where you hve been searching. The best time to see elephant outside their forest stronghold is early in the morning.

10. Food: Be Adventurous!

The larger hotels have first-class restaurants and grill rooms where you can wine and dine in sophisticated air-conditioned comfort, eating meals prepared by excellent cooks. But don't be afraid to sample the traditional dishes of some of Mombasa's varied population. Go to the smaller restaurants in parts of the town off the usual tourist route and try some of the delicious curries, chicken *tika,* prawns *masala* or barbequed beef in tamarind sauce. You will find local people friendly; they will do all they can to help you. You will be surprised how well and how cheaply you can eat out.

On the Island of Mombasa the **Hotel Elias** on the 'S' bend in **Abdel Nasser Road** opposite the market serves a good *biryiani* and mutton *masala.* Tables outside occupied well into the night vouch for its popularity. Up a side road adjacent to Hotel Elias is the **Taj Hotel** with an equally good reputation.

On **Haile Selassie Avenue** is the **Blue Room,** a very popular restaurant serving most of the traditional Indian dishes at very reasonable prices.

Near Sheikh Jundani Mosque the **Hotel Hermes** offers chicken *tika* and curries in clean, air-conditioned surroundings. Try their chicken in coconut milk. It is delicious.

Also in this area is the **Splendid View Café** in **Maungano Road** which is open until midnight, and does 'take away' meals. Most Indian dishes are available, and their shish kebabs are especially recommended. Chinese meals are served in a room upstairs.

The air-conditioned **Shehnai Restaurant,** nearby, serves Muglai dishes to the accompaniment of gentle flute music.

The **Splendid Hotel** itself has a roof which is cool in the hot weather, where oriental food is served.

The **Café Stavrose,** just a step away, makes good *samosas* (spicy curries of meat or vegetable in a light pastry covering) and other snacks are available.

Fish and chips or chicken and chips can be bought at the **Blue Fin Restaurant** which is also close to the Splendid Hotel. The local sea food is excellent.

On **Nkrumah Road,** opposite the Holy Ghost Cathedral, is the

FOOD: BE ADVENTUROUS!

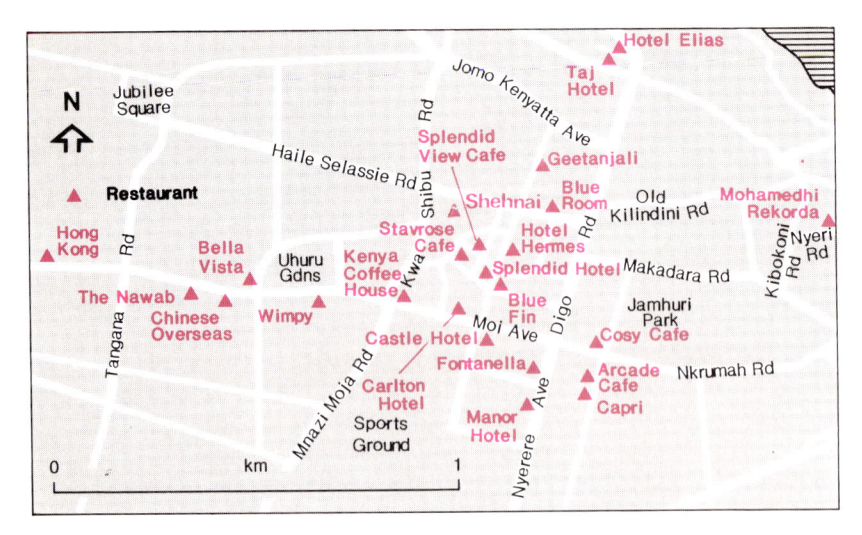

Restaurants in central Mombasa

Cosy Café. Excellent for snacks, their *samosas* [sandwich] are particularly good.

In **Moi Avenue,** a short walk away, there are several eating places. The well-known **Castle Hotel** has a large patio where you can sip a cool drink and watch the world go by. At the back of the building are a pizzeria and the Bui-Bui Bar. The dining room has a fine and varied menu. Almost opposite is the **Carlton Hotel** with a good general menu.

Near the junction of Moi and Nyerere Avenues, in the arcade, is the **Fontanella.** Here you can sit under the shady trees with a tinkling fountain, which is totally unexpected in the heart of the town. The Fontanella is good for ice-cream sodas and light snacks.

Almost next door is the **Manor Hotel,** the oldest in town, where you can sit on a terrace shaded by umbrellas, sip a cooling drink and eat a light meal. It is a convenient meeting place for shoppers. A table d'hote menu of sea foods and meat dishes is served and the prices are reasonable.

For Chinese cuisine try the **Hong Kong Restaurant.** This is much further down Moi Avenue, well past the Tusks. The family who own it have been in Mombasa for many years. The **Florida Night Club** is another of their enterprises. Another good Chinese Restaurant is the **Chinese Overseas Restaurant,** also on Moi Avenue. The **Galaxy** on Haile Selassie Avenue can also be recommended.

FOOD: BE ADVENTUROUS!

The **Bella Vista** behind the Tusks Service Station has a name that belies reality. It serves good curries in clean, air-conditioned surroundings, and the service is efficient.

For a quick snack there is the **Wimpy Bar,** opposite the Tusks, and an ice-cream parlour.

To sample Kenya coffee at its best try the **Kenya Coffee House** in **Motor Mart Building,** or the more peaceful **Arcade Café** in **Ambalal House,** away from the noise of traffic. You may be invited to have coffee at a roadside stall or in an Arab or Indian store. Black coffee spiced with ginger is delicious. Ambalal House also includes the **Capri,** a first-class and very popular air-conditioned restaurant renowned for its steaks.

If you feel truly adventurous, wander off into the winding streets of the **Old Town** one night and sample Arab food. Take the first turning right down Kibokoni Road into **Nyeri Road** and there, with its wooden tables and benches on the pavement, is the **Mohamedhi Rekorda.** Open until 4 a.m. it caters for patrons of the late-night cinemas. Barbequed mutton, beef and chicken with a tamarind sauce are served with the large, soft buns known as *muhamri.* Basic, but fun!

Two recently opened restaurants are **The Nawab** in Moi Avenue opposite UTC, specialising in mughlai dishes and the **Geetanjali** in Msanifu Kombo Street, a vegetarian restaurant specialising in Gujarati, Punjabi and traditional Indian thali dishes.

Leaving the Island and near the old pontoon bridge on **Mainland North** is the **Tamarind.** Here you can enjoy the most enchanting view of the Old Town across the waters of Mombasa Harbour from an open terrace. The setting is memorable, the sea food excellent. A small band plays soft music to complete your evening. Not for disco fans!

Continuing up the Coast road which runs parallel to Kenyatta Beach you come to the turning to **Le Joli Coin** which has a bar and restaurant on the sand. The staff will see that you get a superb meal and advise you on the food. Informal, it is open from early morning breakfast, throughout the day when snacks are available, until dinner time. It is a pleasant spot day or night.

If you are staying on the North Mainland drive over Mtwapa Bridge and visit **Le Pichet,** advertised as the only truly French restaurant. Set on the edge of the Creek, there are pleasant views from the verandah. You can take a trip on a dhow from your hotel and finish up here for lunch.

For an African meal continue up the main road until you reach

FOOD: BE ADVENTUROUS!

Porini Village Restaurant. The speciality is chicken cooked on charcoal, served with a thick tamarind sauce, accompanied by *ugali,* made from maize meal. *Ugali,* beans and cassava form the staple diet of many Africans. The waitresses wear typical Giriama skirts and will bring you a clay pot of water in which to wash your hands before eating.

You may wonder if venison or game-animal meat is available. The **Plaza Hotel** on the **North Coast** serves impala steaks and if you are keen to try game-meat dishes enquire at your hotel. They may be available, though not on the menu. Strange to say, game meat is eaten more on the Continent of Europe than in Africa.

On the South Coast and particularly along the beautiful **Diani Beach** there are several first-class hotels with excellent dining and grill rooms. **Nomad,** to the south of Jadini Hotel, caters especially for visitors. The restaurant and bar are housed in a high *makuti*-roofed building. The floor slopes upwards towards the restaurant, grill and kitchen access at the back. The bar occupies the lower level and is usually crowded with both young and old. Dress is as casual as you like. The sea food is excellent.

A tourist watches while an ngalawa is carefully placed in the shallows on Diani beach

FOOD: BE ADVENTUROUS!

CARNIVORE NAIROBI

A spectacular roast meat feast with the finest selection of venison, meats and poultry. As much as you can eat.

LANGATA ROAD NAIROBI
PHONE 501709 501775/779

— CARNIVORE —
NAIROBI

TAMARIND NAIROBI

The only real seafood restaurant in town. And it's all flown in daily, fresh, from the coast. A meal to remember.

NATIONAL BANK BUILDING
HARAMBEE AVENUE NAIROBI
PHONE 338989 20473

TAMARIND
NAIROBI

TAMARIND MOMBASA

The best seafood restaurant on the coast. Open to sea breezes while you dine and dance under the stars.

NYALI MOMBASA
PHONE 471747 472263

TAMARIND
MOMBASA

SIMBA SALOON NAIROBI

Fun out-of-door atmosphere by night. Dancing Friday and Saturday. Live band Wednesday and Sunday. Informal. family restaurant by day.

CARNIVORE, LANGATA ROAD
PHONE 501709, 501775/779

SIMBA SALOON
NAIROBI

The most difficult choice you'll have to make

So why not try them all?

FOOD: BE ADVENTUROUS!

Viewing the beach at Diani from a parachute drawn by a Land Rover

The only other restaurant not tied to a hotel is on **Wasini Island** and is run by **Thorn Tree Safaris.** Sea food dishes are a speciality. You can join a goggling session with Thorn Tree to Kisite Island, followed by a superb lunch, or you may like to cross to the island from Shimoni by small dhow or motor launch and combine lunch with an exploration of the island.

You may wonder what wines will be available when you dine out. Most hotels carry good stocks of European wines, but because of heavy import duties they tend to be expensive. But study the wine list and you may be able to pick out a reasonable Liebfraumilch or Spanish wine. Kenya beer is excellent and many tourists take to it in a big way!

11. Sports

The Kenya Coast affords opportunities for almost every kind of sport. Apart from swimming in the sea or the pool at your hotel you can enjoy goggling, windsurfing and sailing at speed on a catamaran from most beaches. A few instructors are available to teach scuba diving and for the proficient diver there are several fine areas where most attractive coral gardens and brightly coloured fish are to be seen. Lasers are also popular.

You can water-ski in the sea when it is calm and the **Water Sports Club** in **Rassini Road** makes use of the quiet waters of Tudor Creek (see photograph on title page). Here you can hire a boat to explore the inlets or fish in picturesque surroundings. Coconut plantations on one side and the distant hills beyond make for a peaceful and relaxed outing.

Deep-sea fishing is to some extent seasonal. There are records of many fine catches of sporting fish and enthusiasts come from many countries, returning year after year to try their luck and to renew acquaintance with old friends. The visitor will probably go to the club or establishment nearest to his hotel. There are a great many to choose from.

On the **North Coast** is the **Seahorse** for all water sports and fishing in Kilifi Creek. It has an excellent restaurant.

In **Mtwapa Creek** are **F.G. McConnel** and **James Adcock**, both with a high reputation gained from long experience.

A windsurfing competition off a South Coast beach

On **Kisauni Creek,** facing the Old Town, is the **Bahari Club.** Many boats are moored here and the club has an excellent record.

On **Mombasa Island** there is an old-established firm called **K Boats.** It is near the **Yacht Club** and the entrance to Kilindini Harbour, and hires out boats and crew.

Further south is **Nomad Safaris.** This organization caters for deep-sea fishing and has glass-bottomed boats for visits to the reef and goggling expeditions to nearby islands. On the same beach is a newer enterprise, **Gupta Sea Tours.**

About half an hour's drive from here, at **Shimoni,** is the **Pemba Fishing Club.** It is residential and very efficiently organized, so book early.

For the golfer there is an eighteen-hole course at Nyali and a nine-hole course on the Island. The **Nyali Golf and Country Club** was completed in 1959 as a nine-hole course. In 1980 the course was enlarged to fifteen holes and it now has a full quota of eighteen holes and is up to international standards. Visitors are welcome but should note that on Wednesdays and Thursdays priority is given to four-ball groups and the weekly club competition respectively. It is an interesting course. Ocassionally between shots you can watch monkeys scampering across the fairways to the mango trees, or if you are unlucky, one will pick up your ball. There is an abundance of bird life here too: sometimes the black-headed heron is to be seen, standing statuesquely or more active with a snake in its beak. The Nyali hotels have arrangements with the Club, so enquire at the information desk. Squash and tennis courts are available here, and there is a swimming pool.

The Mombasa Golf Club was founded in 1911 and is the oldest club in Kenya. It has nine holes and is divided into two sections by Mama Ngina Drive. Situated right on the sea front the course has its hazards – one tee requires courage or at least steady nerves as you drive across an inlet where the waves crash against the rocks. It is easy to be distracted by the sight of a large ship sailing in or out of Kilindini Harbour and the views out to sea are magnificent.

Caddies and clubs are obtainable at both courses and the charges are reasonable.

Many hotels have hard courts for tennis and the **Jadini Beach Hotel** on the **South Mainland** has its own pitch and putt golf course. Some hotels have an entertainment officer and games of handball or soccer are arranged on the beach between guests and members of staff.

12. Birds

The visitor cannot avoid noticing the great variety of birds along the Coast, both the colourful and the duller ones. The list that follows is by no means exhaustive and those interested would do well to consult John Williams' *Field Guide to the Birds of East and Central Africa,* or *Birds of Kenya* by John Karmali which is very attractive and informative.

Colourful birds

Weaver birds are common and their nests, so neatly woven in the branches of trees, are to be seen up and down the Coast. It is fascinating to watch the male birds build a hanging nest of palm fronds and then put on a display to attract a female. If unsuccessful the male must build another. Nests are commonly raided by predators such as tree snakes and Indian crows. The latter have been responsible for the disppearance of many small birds from areas of the Coast.

The **lilac breasted roller** is another beautiful, though raucous bird. Its upper feathers are a tawny brown, but when it takes off to fly the wings are a brilliant, irridescent blue and the breast a striking lilac. In flight during the breeding season the male bird rolls from side to side, dipping one wing then the other.

Carmine bee eaters migrate to the Kenya Coast from November to April. They come when bush fires are common and rows of them can be seen on telephone wires above burning grass or bush-land. They dive down through the smoke to catch insects and grasshoppers. These birds have a blue head but the rest of the feathers and long tail are shades of carmine. They usually nest in flocks and when they come to roost the trees at Mida Creek and sites on Kilifi Creek appear to be covered by carmine flowers. They fly off in the morning as though at a word of command and the trees immediately appear dull and colourless.

The **Zanzibar red bishop** is a small bird about the size of a sparrow with black underside feathers, a red cap and brown wing feathers. It is usually found in small flocks. There is a flash of red as the male bird takes off in flight.

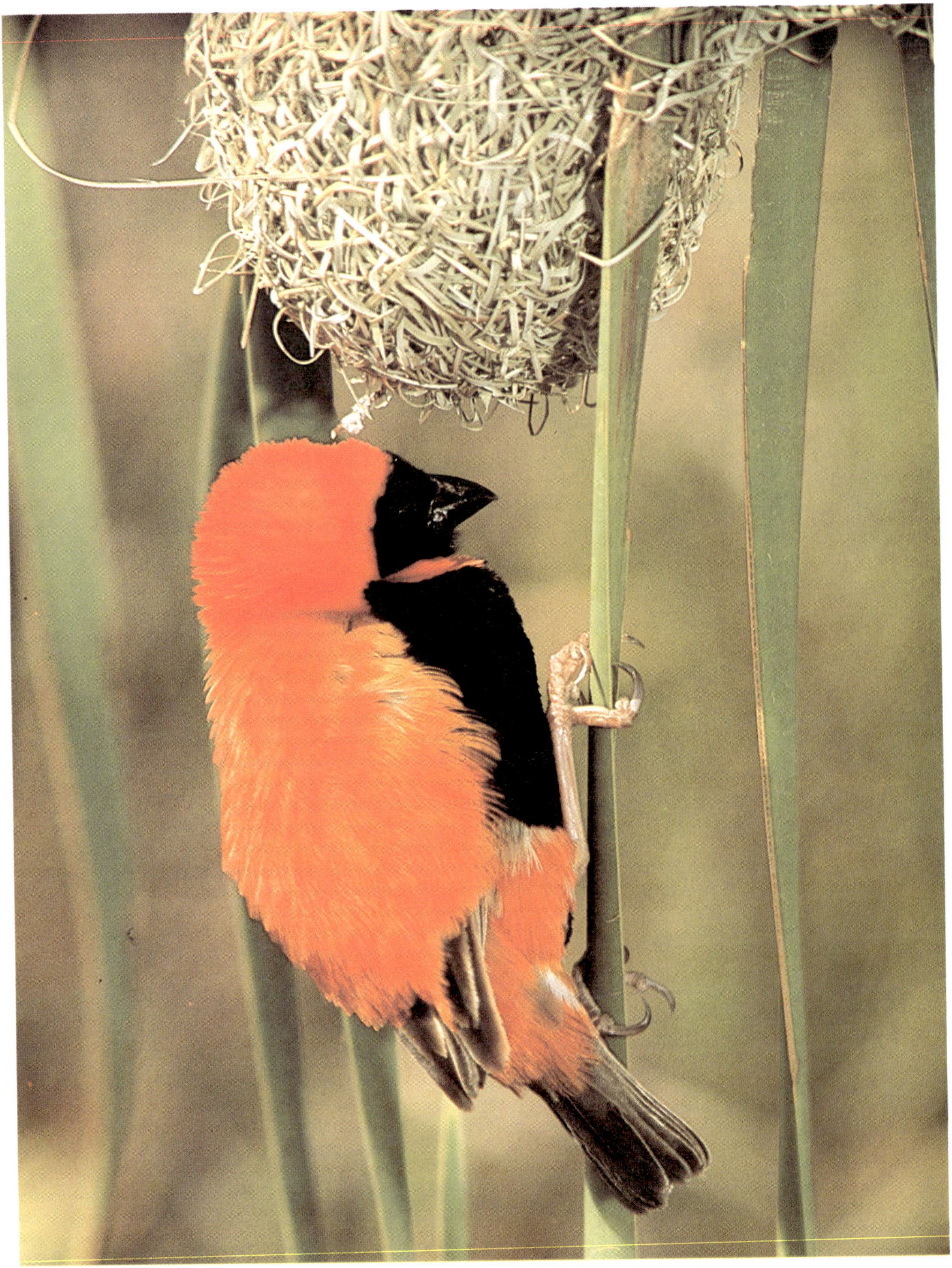

BIRDS

Right: A fish eagle in flight

Below: A golden palm weaver

Opposite: The beautiful southern red bishop

A red-billed hornbill

87

Less common, but very colourful, is the **red-cheeked cordon-bleu.** These birds, smaller than a sparrow, tend to move in flocks. The male has a striking blue plumage and an oval red patch on his cheek. His mate is a duller colour and lacks the red cheek patch.

Tanganyika love birds are quite common and some Coast residents deliberately put out food so that they can have the pleasure of watching them. Their presence is announced by a high-pitched chattering and screeching. There are several varieties. When not feeding they tend to cuddle up together on a branch, talking away and nuzzling their neighbours. They are miniature parrots about 15 centimetres (6 inches) long. The 'yellow collared' variety is the most common. It is mainly green with a dark head and a yellow collar around its neck extending down its back.

Ostriches

Less colourful birds

The **Indian house crow,** it is said, was imported into Zanzibar and East Africa by the Parsi community for their towers of silence. They are aggressive, all-black crows who are cheeky enough to sit on a verandah railing and steal any food left unattended. They have such a variety of raucous calls that one suspects they must have a language. They attack smaller birds and their nests and have been responsible for the migration of many of these species to less vulnerable areas. They even attack pairs of hawks on the wing, when the odds are about twenty to one in their favour. In Mombasa a large number come in to roost near the Railway Station.

The **pied crow** is a larger, but less aggressive bird. It is black with a white chest patch and white nape of the neck. It is far less common than the Indian house crow.

The **drongo** is a black bird about the size of a starling and has a distinctive long, forked tail. It is said to be able to mimic the call of other birds.

The **bulbul** is one of the great morning and evening songsters, not unlike the kiskadee of Guyana. It has a black cap, dark dorsal feathers and a yellow tummy. It is a common visitor to Coastal gardens.

The long-tailed **fiscal shrike** is a bird of character with distinctive black and white markings and a longish tail. Its size is that of a European starling, but it is much trimmer and has a strong, hooked bill. An insect-eater, it is usually seen perched at vantage points, such as branches of trees and telegraph wires, from which to launch itself at its prey. When the hunting is good it provides a larder for itself by impaling its victims on thorns of a convenient bush for later consumption.

The **coucal** is very much like a large thrush, chestnut brown in colour with darker wings and commonly seen hopping from branch to branch in bushes, or perhaps looking for insects on grassy patches close to bushes. Its call resembles the sound of water emptying from an upturned bottle, though it is more melodious. It is often called the 'bottle bird' and, because its call is heard most frequently when rain is about to fall, the 'rain bird'.

If your hotel is on Diani Beach you might easily see the large **silvery cheeked** and **trumpeter hornbills** and hear their loud, coarse calls. Both species enjoy the seeds of the *Mimusops fruticosa* trees close to the beach. The birds are large, mainly

BIRDS

Above: A pied kingfisher

Right: A marabou stork

Right: A black-headed oriole

Below: A white-headed buffalo weaver

Right: A superb starling

black, but with a white underbelly and a large horny protuberance above the beak. A suspicion of silver flecks the cheek of the silvery-cheeked hornbill.

Should you travel up Mtwapa or Kilifi Creeks, or go to Mida Creek, you might see a **pied kingfisher** hovering above the water, its black and white wings quivering before it dives on its prey. It often perches on mangrove branches to study the water for fish. A close relative, the **malachite kingfisher** has bright blue upper feathers and a rufous underside, and a blue and black crest extending backwards from the head.

You may notice a number of brown birds with very long tails perched at the top of bougainvillea bushes. They often take off together when the leader thinks it is time to try another bush. These are **mouse birds.**

There are several varieties of **gulls, herons** and **egrets,** some of which are migrant birds, and these can be seen on the reefs and beaches. It is interesting to note that the gulls always seem to fly against the prevailing monsoon. Perhaps this helps them pick up smells on the wind which might indicate fish or other food ahead.

One of the heron family, the **black-headed heron,** is frequently seen inland from the beaches and is quite common on Nyali Golf Course. It hunts a number of small creatures – rats, field mice and snakes, and can sometimes be seen standing absolutely still and poised before darting its beak down to capture its prey.

Mida Creek is outside the scope of this book, being north of Kilifi, but it is an excellent bird-watching site.

Scared ibis perched high in a tree

13. Trees and Flowering Shrubs

When you first arrive in Mombasa you will probably be intrigued by the sight of thatched cottages, waving palm trees and brilliant blues and greens of the sea. Later on you may be enchanted by the colourful trees and bushes around the Kenya Coast. Some of the commoner trees and shrubs will be described briefly to help you identify them. The Swahili name is given in most cases, in brackets afterwards.

Trees

The Baobab (mbuyu)
This weird-looking tree is seen up and down the Coast, its habitat extending about 200 kilometres (124 miles) inland. It develops a huge rounded trunk as it ages and has branches which, minus leaves, resemble roots. This gives rise to the legend that the Almighty planted the tree upside down. It has a large white flower and the ovoid fruit contains cream of tartar. Near the ferry, on the Island side, you can see the remains of what was once a large forest of baobabs. (It was also the site of an ancient village.) The flower buds attract both bush babies and colobus monkeys.

The Sausage Tree (mwegea)
A small tree, but quite unmistakable with its large, light green fruit, shaped like huge sausages. The fruit is inedible even to monkeys; the attractive purple flower blooms only at night and has an unpleasant scent. The fruit is fermented to produce an alcoholic drink, but the taste is definitely an acquired one.

The Nandi Flame (mkifabakazi)
From July to October these beautiful trees produce large orange-red flowers which are most strikingly framed by their dark green leaves. They are tall trees, reaching up some 12 to 15 metres (40 or 50 feet) in height and when the flowers fall they stand on a carpet of red. They grow in the towns and the countryside.

TREES AND FLOWERING SHRUBS

TREES AND FLOWERING SHRUBS

Opposite: Coconut vendor at top of tree collecting nuts

Right: An umbrella shaped thorn tree, at Tsavo West National Park

Below: A flamboyant tree in full bloom

Left: A baobab tree. Its large, drooping white flowers develop into oval fruit which contains cream of tartar

TREES AND FLOWERING SHRUBS

The Flamboyant (mkakaya)
This is another lovely tree when in flower, usually around Christmas time and extending into April. Most of the year its branches are bare apart from hundreds of long, black seed pods. When the feathery green leaves appear, followed by the brilliant scarlet flowers, the trees seem to be aflame with colour. Not very tall, it is usually umbrella-shaped.

Palm Trees
These are abundant in many varieties, the most ubiquitous being the **coconut palm,** *mnazi,* with so many uses for the local population.

Unripe nuts provide a cool, nutritious drink known as *madafu;* palm toddy is made by fermenting the juice extracted from the shoots near the developing flower. Mature coconut, *nazi,* is used for cooking (as coconut milk); dried and pulped inner coconut is made into oil and soap. Remnants of the dessicated coconut, after milk has been taken out, are used in the manufacture of soap; the hard shell for fuel. The leaves are used for roofing (*makuti*) and can be seen at the Coast on huts and hotels. The outer fibrous cover makes rope.

The **doum palm,** whose branches bifurcate at regular intervals, support bunches of small orange-coloured nuts. The fruit is very fibrous and tastes bitter, but African children and adults enjoy them.

There are many ornamental palms. The tall, straight one with a neat cluster of leafy branches at the top is the Royal Palm, *mvumo,* probably the doyen of them all. Close to the water's edge the *borassus palm* seems to flourish as does the screw pine which grows to about 9 metres (30 feet) and has the most remarkable fruits and roots.

The **traveller's palm,** misnamed because it is really of the banana family, is truly distinctive, being shaped like a large fan. Water collects where the leaves join the stem, thus giving the plant its name. It is also said that the palm fans out from east to west, another aid to travellers. However, two trees growing close to one another will often disprove this belief.

The Indian Almond Tree (mkungu)
These very fine trees can grow up to a height of 18 metres (60 feet). They are at their most attractive around August and September when the large green leaves turn a deep red and later fall to the

ground. New green leaves form almost immediately. The ovoid fruit appears at this time, purple and about the size of a tennis ball. Africans enjoy eating the rather stringy flesh and if you crack open the nut there is a small kernel which tastes like an almond.

The Cashew Nut Tree (Mkanju); nuts (korosho)

All along the Coast are plantations of these small trees, interspersed with coconut palms. They are leafy trees and in season produce a fleshy, bell-shaped fruit, the nut protruding from the end. The fruit is sometimes used to make a sauce. The nuts are difficult to extract from their hard outer covering, and when grown commercially are sent to the Cashew Nut Factory at Kilifi for extraction and grading for sale. Cashew nuts are extremely popular with an evening drink.

The Mango Tree (mwembe)

Very common along the Coast, the mango has an abudance of glossy green leaves on widely-spreading branches. It grows quickly and is a useful shade tree as well as producing delicious fruit. Locals eat mangoes green, with salt, as well as ripe ones.

The larger, graded mangoes from Malindi and Lamu are delicious and can taste similar to a peach. Some, however, are stringy and taste something like paraffin. One district of Mombasa is called *Mwembe Tayari* – ripe mango.

The Casuarina (mvinje)

This tree occurs frequently on the beach. It is tall and slender with delicate, ferny branches and prickly small cones which are painful to tread on. The trunks are occasionally used for masts. They grow well at the Coast, and at the Bamburi Reclamation Area the forest of trees has required almost no soil.

The Kapok Tree (msufi)

Large numbers of these grow on the south coast, and just beyond the bridge over the Tiwi River is a factory producing kapok, still used for stuffing pillows and mattresses. The trees are tall and their branches come off almost horizontally in groups, the large pods at the ends. When these pods burst the white fluffy kapok is blown like thistledown on the wind.

TREES AND FLOWERING SHRUBS

The Neem Tree (msubili, or mwitu)
A fairly common leafy tree with small, pale green leaves and clusters of yellow, pea-sized fruit in season. The delicate, small white flowers are strongly scented and are said to cause hay fever. The neem grows quickly and makes a fine shade tree. A branch put among clothing in cupboards is reputed to keep off moths.

The Cassia Tree (Latin: Cassia Fistula)
When in flower this small tree is completely clothed in cascades of yellow. It is very striking at the roadside. When not in bloom it is a rather uninteresting tree with long seed pods. It is reminiscent of the European laburnum.

The Geranium Tree
Down the centre of many dual carriageways you will see lines of small trees with fairly large, oval green leaves and small red flowers. These are the geranium trees whose hardiness have made them so suitable for roadway decoration.

A travellers' palm among canna lilies. A mango tree on left

Right and below left: Two varieties of hibiscus

Centre right: The delicate heavily-scented frangipani

Right: Brilliant yellow cassia fistula tree in full bloom

Flowering shrubs

The Desert Rose (msanapiti)
With stem and branches looking like a miniature baobab, the desert rose has trumpet-shaped flowers of deep pink or red, protruding through their covering of dark green leaves. The flowers are prominent as the leaves wither. It used to be a great joy to come across one of these bushes while driving through a dusty brown game reserve. But many have been uprooted to enhance the beauty of gardens at coastal hotels and game lodges.

The Hibiscus
This is another shrub with a delicate beauty. The most commonly seen is bright scarlet, but in private gardens you find pale yellow, cream, pink or mixed shades in blossom. The flower is bell-shaped and opens wide during the day, its yellow anther protruding well beyond the petals. One variety, the sleeping hibiscus, as the name suggests never opens fully. A particularly lovely blossom is the double hibiscus which is like a fully-blown rose. The flowers last for one day.

Helvetia and Alamanda
These are to be seen decorating central islands and roundabouts in town for they have long-lasting, bright yellow blossoms. There are many varieties, some grow into small trees and can be trimmed into shape, others grow in profusion on walls.

The Bougainvillea
A joy to behold, this brilliant flower with its bracts of purple, red, orange or white stands up to the hottest sun and needs little moisture. One variety, known as 'Mary Palmer', has red, white and mottled red-white mixed bracts on the same plant and is truly spectacular. Bougainvilleas are very adaptable and can be trimmed into standards, kept low on wires, or left to riot gloriously over walls.

14. Suggested Tours

Gedi

The Gedi ruins are well worth a visit. They lie close to the **Malindi road** some 105 kilometres (65 miles) from Mombasa. It is a good idea to plan your visit as part of a trip to Watamu or Malindi. For a photographer an afternoon visit is better than one in the morning.

Gedi represents what is left of an Arab colonial town of the fifteenth century which was quite suddenly deserted in the seventeenth century for reasons that are not clear. The town may have been overrun by the warlike Galla during their migration south. Another theory is that its water supply was cut off by a change in course of the Sabaki River, probably Gedi's main water supply.

The ruins at Gedi

SUGGESTED TOURS

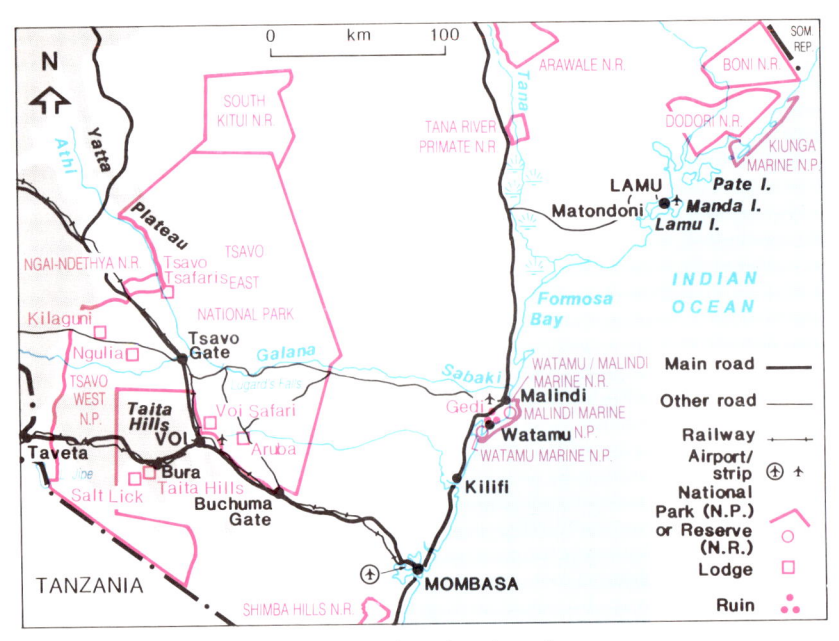

Tours and national parks

The town is enclosed within two walls and all the important buildings are within the inner wall. The remains of the magnificent entrance to the palace, its other doorways and those into the great mosque indicate that Gedi was a town of some opulence. James Kirkman, who was responsible for clearing the site and investigating the archaeological remains, has named all the important buildings. The 'house of the scissors', the 'house of the Chinese cash' and the 'house of the ivory box' are some of the intriguing places to visit. The 'plumbing' and drainage systems are also interesting.

A strange thing about Gedi is that the Portuguese and Arabs did not mention it in their writings. It probably had a different name when people lived there. Kirkman thinks it might have been 'Quelman' which appears on an old map and may be a rendering of the Swahili *Kilimani* – the 'place on the hill'.

Europeans visiting the site in the early 1920s commented on a distinctly ghostly feeling about the place. Today the sense of ghostly oppression no longer exists.

James Kirkman's booklet about Gedi can be bought at the entrance gate and will help to bring to life the remains of this enigmatic city.

SUGGESTED TOURS

Top: Camels being exercised along a beach

Lower picture: Sailing craft beached at Malindi, mainly mashua, with a jahazi to the left

Malindi

Malindi has experienced periods of prosperity as a bustling Arab township and great poverty when it was almost deserted. It is now an attractive seaside resort with several hotels lining the foreshore. There are three distinct areas in the town: the seaside hotels and a new shopping centre to the north, the Old Town in the centre which reaches from Lawford's Hotel to Vasco da Gama Point, then a long stretch of beach, Silversands, with hotels and seaside accommodation and several private homes to the south. further south is **Casuarina Point,** beyond which is the **Malindi Marine National Park.** This extends from Casuarina Point to Malindi Point with the North Reef and Leopard Reef as the seaward boundary. It forms the northern part of the much larger Marine National Reserve reaching south from Vasco da Gama Point to just beyond Mida Creek. You can go by glass-bottomed boat out into the Park and see a wonderful variety of colourful coral heads and fishes; the boat stops for a goggling session. Goggling, even if you are unable to dive and have to float on the surface, is most rewarding. It is wise to wear plastic sandals because you often want to touch down and stand while you look around and coral can be very sharp.

The northern hotels are all modern with high-class accommodation and most have swimming pools. The catering is good. The earliest was the **Blue Marlin** (originally Palm Beach Hotel), followed by **Lawford's** (set up by a retired district officer, Commander Lawford, in 1934). The **Sinbad** with its attractive Arab architecture was also early on the scene. Since these pioneers Malindi has become a very popular resort and many new hotels have sprung up with a shopping centre, banks and a night-club behind them. There is a long stretch of beach with sand dunes on its northern part. It is flat and a big expanse of sand is uncovered at low tide. During the northern monsoon the beach takes on a rusty hue due to the silt swept down by the Sabaki River. Because there is a break in the reef quite large surfing rollers follow one another and crash close to the water's edge. Enthusiasts get a lot of fun riding these waves on their surfboards.

Between the hotels and the Old Town the roadside is lined by small stalls selling Akamba carvings, basket ware, bead necklaces and many other items of local make. You are liable to be brought under pressure to buy, but don't take the persuasive sales talk too seriously.

The Old Town consists of the usual cluster of *dukas* – small shops selling a great variety of goods. Malindi is famous for its *halwa*, the local 'Turkish Delight'. The best place to get it is at Balawy and Sons in Odinga Street.

The District Commissioner's house is not unlike the ruined one in Shimoni and dates from 1890, but it is in a reasonable state of repair. Close to it was a memorial erected by the Portuguese Government to commemorate the five hundredth anniversary of the death of Prince Henry the Navigator. Vasco da Gama's voyage and the pilot who guided him to Goa, Ibn Majid, are also commemorated. If you walk past the DC's house towards the sea you will find a mosque with two ancient pillar tombs. On the sea front you will find the Fish Market and close to it there are usually a number of fishing boats, Lamu *jahazis* and smaller native craft. At the end of this beach you will see the **Vasco da Gama cross,** erected in 1499, and a boat-repair area on the beach.

South of the Vasco da Gama cross is **Silversands,** a long stretch of beach with a variety of beach accommodation and private houses. The **Driftwood Beach Club** is not far beyond the central part of this beach and is very popular with the younger set. Lunches and dinners are well prepared and served; crab, lobster and prawn are mouth-watering specialities.

Another excellent eating place, especially for a day visitor, is the **Umande.** *Umande* means 'dew' but the word is also used for the early morning land breeze. It is 3 kilometres (nearly 2 miles) south of Malindi on the road to Casuarina Point: road signs will guide you to it. The current proprietor has a fine reputation for the loving care he puts into producing delicious meals.

Watamu

To get to Watamu, take the turning to Gedi and travel seaward. The road leads towards a headland with **Blue Lagoon** to the north and **Turtle Bay** to the south. Some of the small, rounded coral islands in the bay resemble turtle shells at high tide, hence the name. There are several hotels, and of these **Ocean Sports** and **Seafarers** cater especially for those who want to go goggling near the reef or deep-sea fishing. Their seafood can be recommended. Beyond the hotels are private houses; further south is the entrance to **Mida Creek** which is locally famous for its bird life. Many varieties of seabirds and migrating birds nest there. Trips to Mida

SUGGESTED TOURS

Above: The waterfront at Lamu

Right: Donkeys carrying loads along the narrow streets of Lamu

Creek with an ornithologist are arranged fairly frequently and your hotel may have information about them.

Lamu

Lamu is a small, old Arab town on an island of that name about 350 kilometres (217 miles) north of Mombasa, largely unspoilt by the encroachment of modern civilization. A good way to get there is by local bus from Mombasa. This can be tiring, but it will give you a chance to see a number of different places of interest on the way. The bus does not go when the rains are heavy and the Tana River is overflowing its banks. The most comfortable way is to go by air. The airfield is on Manda Island and you cross to Lamu in a motor boat or small motorized dhow. Those with plenty of time may like to go by dhow from Mombasa's Old Port. Recently an amphibian seaplane capable of taking four passengers started to fly from Kilifi.

Lamu is one of the Bajun Islands which include the most northerly, Kiwayu – a long, thin strip of land with a rounded, cleft north-eastern tip – Ndau, Pate and Manda, going south. In earlier days there was a good deal of rivalry between the sheikhs of Pate and Lamu. Today the free and easy life-style of Lamu attracts a great variety of people – some of whom Lamu could perhaps do without.

Lamu town is fascinating from many points of view. Its narrow streets, old Arab-style houses walled in with a small garden and well, its market and the shops, will enchant you. The **Old Fort**, with the open market square in front, is almost the central feature of the town. A walk up the hill to the **Riyadha Mosque**, famed world-wide for its part in the *Maulidi* celebrations (Maulidi is celebrated as the Prophet's birthday), through narrow lanes with perhaps donkeys to squeeze past, will give you a superb view of the sea front and roof-tops of the town. You will find the people very friendly.

A stroll along the waterfront at any time of the day is most rewarding. The style of the buildings is unique and their fine Arab doors outstanding. There are several along the waterfront and many more in the town. The wood is delicately carved around the door and the central, vertical beam which is of some size is always highly decorated with carved patterns and large brass spikes as part of the decoration. Such a door is impressive on any house.

The Lamu dhows, both sailing and motorized, ply to and from the waterfront while others are anchored close to the sea-wall. They take passengers to Shela, Matondoni or across to Manda Island and some are engaged in bringing in *boriti* (mangrove poles) to be stacked ready for transport elsewhere. *Ngalawas* and other small *daus* make a colourful scene lying hauled up on the beach.

Lamu Museum is on the waterfront and is a 'must'. The fascinating exhibits include rooms demonstrating the rituals of a bride and groom's traditional wedding, sailing craft, porcelain ware and locally – made furniture.

Petley's Inn is part of Lamu's recent history, and being centrally placed on the waterfront everything happens around it. Their advertisement says, 'The original Petley's was oft quoted as being quite the worst hotel in the world, and Percy Petley as being without rival the worst hotelier in the world'. Today it is a meeting place for young and old of many communities.

Shela is a small fishing village to seaward of Lamu and you can walk to it from Lamu in half an hour. It is more fun, perhaps, to sail in a *mashua* or small Lamu dhow and enjoy the views of both sides of the creek. Its former importance is reflected in a number of impressive houses. Most of these have tumbled into a state of decay, but recently many have been bought up and renovated.

Peponi Hotel is on the waterfront and can be recommended as a seaside hotel with a vast stretch of clean, sandy beach extending to seaward and around the sea frontage of the Island. Coming in to the beach in a *mashua*, the hotel with the old mosque behind it is a very attractive scene.

If you stay here for a few days, trips to the **Takwa Ruins** on **Manda Island** and up to **Matondoni** where the Lamu *jahazis* are constructed are interesting outings. A visit further afield to **Pate Island** with its ancient history will give you an insight into the rivalries of past centuries.

Game park tours and lodges

Kenya abounds in a variety of game parks. The following is a brief account of those nearest to the Coast. However, you can fly to distant areas such as the Mara where some of the finest game parks or reserves are located.

Voi Safari Lodge
This is the nearest lodge to Mombasa and is a short distance inside the **Voi Gate** of the **East Tsavo Park.** Coming by road you may go in at the **Buchuma Gate,** less than 100 kilometres (62 miles) from Mombasa. Travelling through the Park you will probably see a variety of animals on your way to the Lodge. You will very likely pass **Aruba Dam** and Lodge and may like to stop here for a cool drink and a stroll down to the water's edge where there is a tremendous variety of water birds. A tree on a small island in the dam is only about 50 metres from the edge and is often covered with birds. If you are lucky you will see elephant or buffalo coming to water. Waterbuck, impala and Grant's Gazelle are usually close by and if you are really lucky you may see lions on a kill. They tend to keep close to waterholes, especially during dry periods, in the expectation that their prey will come to them. When they have young they do not relish having to travel far. This expanse of water is mainly artificial, having been created by damming the Voi River. The Lodge is on a 'do-it-yourself' basis: you bring your own food to cook.

Voi Safari Lodge is one of the most attractive in Kenya, set on a hillside overlooking one natural waterhole and two artificial ones. The Lodge has been built to blend with the colouring of the hillside. There is a hide like a military pillbox close to one of the artificial waterholes which is fed by the cleanest water and is the ultimate choice of elephant and buffalo, even though they may make a start at the natural waterhole. The hide is approached by a hidden stairway and sometimes the animals are so close you could almost touch them. The Lodge has a swimming pool and the catering and bar facilities are good.

One of the things that strikes you, looking out from the Lodge, is the vastness of the Park laid out before you. The flat plain, studded with thorn trees, extends to the distant Yatta Plateau and on either side are volcanic sugar loaf hills of some magnitude. During dry seasons, huge herds of elephant and buffalo can be watched as they approach the waterhole – the buffalo usually give way to the elephant.

Taita Hills Lodge and Salt Lick
These lodges come under the same general management and are situated near the road to Taveta. You take the Taveta Road at Voi, a turning at right angles to the Mombasa – Nairobi Road, which

SUGGESTED TOURS

Above: The mosque at Shela with Manda Island in the background

Visiting Akamba dancers wearing Colobus monkey skin head-dresses

SUGGESTED TOURS

Left: A giraffe browsing in a road in Tsavo West National Park with tick birds busy on his back

Below: Peponi Hotel at Shela, Lamu Island. Its almost deserted beach extends seawards round the entrance to Lamu's anchorage

is the highway to Moshi in Tanzania. The turn to the Lodges is about 40 kilometres (25 miles) from Voi. You travel at first through sisal plantations and then at Bura the impressive Taita Hills are close by to your right. To your left the landscape was the scene of several battles during the 1914-18 war when Von Lettow Vorbeck attempted to cut the Uganda Railway lines and so disrupt rail traffic between Mombasa and Nairobi.

The **Taita Hills Lodge** never fails to impress the visitor. Approaching the entrance are large, multicoloured beds of low-cut bougainvillea. The whole building is a riot of colour, with bougainvillea climbing all over it and hiding the walls. The main building has been constructed by piling up layers of sand and cement bags. The reception and main lounge has a high ceiling with seating arranged round a central fireplace under a conical chimney. The whole decor, from the trench-like sandbags of the outer walls, is based on effecting a First World War German scene. There are a swimming pool, camels to give you a jerky ride, and marvellous views of the Taita Hills. For game viewing you should go to Salt Lick. Even if you are booked at Salt Lick you lunch at Taita Hills Lodge before proceeding to your destination.

Salt Lick has been cleverly constructed so that the bedrooms look like two-storeyed *makuti*-roofed huts on stilts. Each pair of rooms stands on a cylindrical support which takes waterpipes to the rooms and waste pipes away from them. The rooms stretch out like arms from the central building with dining rooms, bar and areas for watching the waterholes. The waterholes are fairly near the main central building, but there is also a close-up pillbox reached by walking along a covered passage. The area used to contain a lot of salt, being at the edge of a shallow lake in prehistoric times. It also appears to be on the course of an elephant migration. As with a lot of waterholes, the number of animals you see there varies. Recent rains often keep them away from waterholes such as this one.

A drive around the Park area may bring you to battle sites of the First World War as well as showing you animals. Notice boards at the Lodges show the positions of recent animal sightings.

Ngulia and Kilaguni Lodges

These lodges in West Tsavo Park are a good deal further away from Mombasa than the Voi and Taita Hill Lodges. Travelling by road from Mombasa the shortest distance is by entering the

Park through the **Tsavo River Gate.** If time is short you can fly to each of these Lodges from Mombasa or Diani; each has an airstrip. Once there, trips can be arranged to places in the Park like **Mzima Springs.**

Ngulia Lodge is sited at the head of the Ngulia Valley with views to one side of the towering and craggy range of the same name which is 1821 metres (6000 feet) high. A steep drop on the other side looks across to the **Yatta Plateau.** A stream runs through the valley and the Lodge has its own waterhole. There is a small source of fresh water with salted grass around it within metres of the spacious verandah and dining room. Elephant often drink and splash water over themselves at the main pool before slowly ambling up to the salt licks very close to the hotel. Buffalo, waterbuck and jackals are common. This is an attractive lodge architecturally and has an added bonus for bird-watchers because it is on the migration route and the night lights attract many birds towards the Lodge. The road up the valley to the Lodge runs close to two rocky outcrops and if you look carefully you have a good chance of seeing a klipspringer, a very dainty miniature antelope, standing statuesquely on a small rocky projection.

Where the valley expands at the bottom of the gorge you can see another Lodge perched on the hillside just above a small waterhole. Like Aruba, this is a 'do-it-yourself' lodge. **Kilanguni Lodge** is more westward and further from the main road. The original lodge, now the central feature, overlooks a very ancient waterhole to which animals have come for centuries. It is so placed on the slope above the waterhole that you get magnificent views of the peaks of Kilimanjaro in the distance. The Chyulu Hills to your right and the sugar loaf hills to your left are eloquent reminders of volcanic upheavals in prehistoric times. The Lodge has been expanded to either side of the original building with a swimming pool and other facilities within the walled compound. The airstrip is close to the back of the Lodge complex.

A smaller waterhole is sited between the main one below and the Lodge, and salt is scattered on the ground close to the viewing verandah. Animals approach the waterhole from all directions and herds of zebra and impala often come close. There is a large rubbing stone adjacent to the nearer waterhole where an elephant will go through a pantomime of movements to get rid of that intolerable itch. Elephants may stroll up to within yards of the Lodge to sample the salt. Even when animals are scarce the bird life is plentiful and many of the less shy species are attracted to the

SUGGESTED TOURS

An elephant enjoying a rubbing stone at Voi Safari Lodge

Water holes at Voi Safari Lodge where buffalo and elephant sometimes dispute their rights

SUGGESTED TOURS

Above: Taita Hills Lodge, its facade covered with bougainvillea in many colours

Right: A young male bushbuck at the Bamburi Nature Trail

raised ledge of the viewing-base by plates containing left-overs of the last meal. Families of hyrax, the rock rabbit, also take their share of the proffered food.

A trip to **Mzima Springs** will round off your stay at Tsavo. The Springs are not far from Kilaguni and their water, which bubbles out of the volcanic rock, has been Mombasa's main supply for many years. In the deep water of the pools formed above the river, which runs away to join the Tsavo River, you will always see hippo. These large animals can be extremely entertaining. You may see them walking on the bottom of the pool, surfacing for a breather and giving you a dentist's view of their huge teeth, or squabbling with one another in loud grunts. Crocodiles are common on the opposite bank and impala, bushbuck and other antelope come here to water. There is a fascinating underwater tank where you can watch *tilapia* and other fish which often seem as curious to view you as you are to view them.

15. A few Swahili words

Swahili is the lingua franca of the East African Coast. Learn a few words and you will be rewarded with added respect. (The pronunciation is similar to that of the Latin languages.)

Welcome	*Karibu*
please	*tafadhali*
thank you	*ahsante*
today	*leo*
tomorrow	*kesho*
yesterday	*jana*
right	*kulia*
left	*kushoto*
cold	*baridi*
hot	*moto*
to eat	*kula*
to drink	*kunywa*
bread	*mkate*
butter	*siagi*
meat	*nyama*
fish	*samaki*
salt	*chumvi*
pepper	*pilipili*
water	*maji*
tea	*chai*
coffee	*kahawa*
milk	*maziwa*
cup	*kikombe*
plate	*sahani*
knife	*kisu*
fork	*uma*
spoon	*kijiko*
glass (tumbler)	*bilauri*
to sleep	*kulala*
to wake	*kuamka*
toilet/lavatory	*choo*
quickly	*upesi*
slowly	*pole pole*
let's go	*twende*
good-bye	*kwaheri*

(Your host will probably reply *Karibu*, meaning 'Come again')

1	*moja*	15	*kumi na tano*
2	*mbili*	16	*kumi na sita*
3	*tatu*	17	*kumi na saba*
4	*nne*	18	*kumi na nane*
5	*tano*	19	*kumi na tisa*
6	*sita*	20	*ishirini*
7	*saba*	30	*thelathini*
8	*nane*	40	*arobaini*
9	*tisa*	50	*hamsini*
10	*kumi*	60	*sitini*
11	*kumi na moja*	70	*sabini*
12	*kumi na mbili*	80	*themanini*
13	*kumi na tatu*	90	*tisini*
14	*kumi na nne*	100	*mia moja*

Above: Egrets, herons and other water birds roosting at Aruba Dam, Tsavo East National Park

Right: A dainty, rarely seen klipspringer in Tsavo West National Park

Right: Lions after a kill

Below: Farms in the Taita Hills

Acknowledgements:

In preparing the text for this Guide Book I am indebted to many friends who have given me information and opinions which have been invaluable to me. It is difficult to pick out names for special mention. Mrs Lorna Hayes, Chairperson of the Coast Tourist Association, with her wide knowledge of the tourist scene has been especially kind in this respect. My wife Madelon and Mrs Ferial Lowe have been responsible for the typescript. Nothing could have been submitted without their help and suggestions.

J.H.A. Jewell

For permission to reproduce photographs, the publishers are grateful to Ardea for page 86; to John Budds for page 77; to Vincent Oliver for page 55; to Colin Wadhams for page 10, and page 99, top and centre photographs; and to John Jewell for all the remaining pages, including the cover photograph.

4261-5
5-13